GIUSEPPE VERDI

POCKET
GIANTS

GIUSEPPE
VERDI

POCKET
GIANTS

DANIEL
SNOWMAN

Cover image © Mary Evans Picture Library

First published 2014

The History Press
The Mill, Brimscombe Port
Stroud, Gloucestershire, GL5 2QG
www.thehistorypress.co.uk

British Library Cataloguing in Publication Data.
A catalogue record for this book is available from the British Library.

ISBN 978 0 7524 9325 1

Typesetting and origination by The History Press
Printed in Europe

Contents

1

Giant of History

I was taken to my first opera by my father. It was a week or so before my ninth birthday and the opera was Verdi's *Rigoletto*, a rip-roaring work about sex and murder, two topics I did not yet know much about! However, I was perfectly capable of recognising big, bold passions as they came pouring across the footlights and, to this day, well over two-thirds of a century later, I still recall the overwhelming impact of my first exposure to this most ambitious and multimedia of art forms. The extravagant sets and colourful costumes, the big theatrical gestures and passionately projected voices, and above all Verdi's energised, dynamic music with its muscular mix of bravado and pathos, ecstasy and anger, tears and ultimate tragedy: I devoured them all. During the first interval, my father turned to me, gently asking whether I had had enough and would I like him to take me home? No, I exclaimed with mock resentment, I do *not* want to be taken home, adding: 'We haven't even got to the bit that I know from *your* gramophone records: *La donna è mobile!*' That night, I laughed with the lascivious duke, loved with the vulnerable Gilda and wept at the end with her bitter, bereaved father. Today, well over a thousand opera performances later, I still find myself deeply moved by a great performance of a great opera such as *Rigoletto*.

Opera is the art form which, historically, emerged from the attempt in late Renaissance Italy to combine and integrate all the others. Most of the operas produced in the centuries since have fallen by the wayside with only a tiny number – forty or fifty perhaps from among the many thousands that have been written – consistently retaining a place in the worldwide repertoire. Operas by Meyerbeer, once popular, are nowadays rarely performed, while some by Handel, long disregarded as unperformable on stage, have recently enjoyed an unaccustomed place in the operatic sun. A handful of composers (Bizet, Gounod, Mascagni, Leoncavallo) cling to operatic immortality primarily because of a single work that has managed to retain its popularity. But who can be said to have contributed a number of works to the universally accepted operatic repertoire? Mozart and Puccini certainly; Rossini, Donizetti and Richard Strauss probably. And then come the giants, Wagner and Verdi. Of this select band, probably the most widely performed, from his day to ours, is Giuseppe Verdi. My father was right to take me to *Rigoletto*, an opera that remains a mainstay of every self-respecting company in the world and has done so consistently ever since its 1851 premiere. Much the same is true of *La traviata* or works such as *Il trovatore* and *Aida*.

Ambitious Verdi operas such as *Don Carlos, Un ballo in maschera, La forza del destino* and *Simon Boccanegra*, all of them packed with poignant, lyrical beauty punctuated by big-scene grandeur, continue to receive new productions in the opera houses of the world, while Verdi's final works for the stage, *Otello* and *Falstaff*, two masterpieces with nothing in common except their Shakespearean inspiration, each provide a supremely powerful theatrical experience when produced with a cast capable of doing them justice.

But Verdi is not just a giant of operatic history or a massively creative artist. He also grew to become a giant figure in the history of his nation. When Italy achieved unity and statehood for the first time in 1861, Verdi was invited to become a deputy in the first all-Italian parliament and later made a senator for life. On his death in 1901, the old man was universally mourned as the supreme embodiment of the nation he had helped create, a beloved national treasure comparable with that other crusty octogenarian, Queen Victoria, who had passed away a few days before. A month later, as vast crowds poured into the streets of Milan to witness his progress to his final resting place, many people throughout Italy felt that Verdi's importance to his country was as potent as his importance to his art.

***

Verdi died in the Gran Hotel et de Milan, just up the road from La Scala, on 27 January 1901. During his final decline, the city authorities covered the streets outside his hotel room with straw to dull the sound of horses' hooves, and people began to congregate nearby as their beloved maestro sank gradually towards his inevitable demise. On the day of the funeral, as the cortege wound its way across Milan, the largest crowds the city had ever witnessed lined the route. Gently and spontaneously, they began to sing the chorus *Va pensiero* (from his opera *Nabucco*), Verdi's paean to his beloved homeland penned nearly sixty years earlier as a coded anthem yearning for a united, independent Italy.

Thus the legend. And, like most legends, or clichés, it contains an element of truth. In fact, Verdi's actual funeral was, as he had instructed, a relatively modest affair and he was initially buried in Milan's Cimitero Monumentale. But a month later, to great pomp and circumstance, his body was transferred to lie (alongside that of his wife) across town in the crypt of the Casa di Riposo, the home for retired musicians that Verdi himself had founded and funded. As the cortege was about to leave the Cimitero, Arturo Toscanini, the 33-year-old principal conductor at La Scala, led a huge choir in a performance of *Va pensiero*. Some of those within earshot doubtless sang along, though press reports suggest the overall impact was diluted by the vast open-air space the choir had to fill –

and the prolonged whistle of a locomotive at the nearby train station.[1] As for the suggestion that this chorus was a surrogate national hymn – this may have been a common perception by 1901, but was hardly that back in 1842 when it was composed.

Much that happened in Verdi's life remains clouded by myth or uncertainty, and the man himself, like many ageing celebrities, was not above adding to the mystique. 'I am just a peasant, rough-hewn,'[2] he would chuckle to visitors, seeming to forget that his father, Carlo Verdi, ran an inn, kept efficient accounts and, in a society in which most were illiterate, could read and write and afford to send his son to school. True, the family background was provincial, living as they did in a tiny village near what was a smallish town, but that was true of most Italians in those days. Different parts of the vast Italian peninsula were ruled by a series of remote, often foreign-based authorities whose writ tended to impinge upon village life far less directly than that of the landowners and priesthood of the vicinity. Life was, essentially, lived in the locality, with local people, local diet and local dialect. Even into old age, long after Italy had been united and its national language standardised, Verdi spoke and wrote Italian with occasional imperfections deriving from the regional dialect he had learned as a youngster.[3] 'Just a peasant'? No. But one can see why the wealthy celebrity of the 1870s and 1880s, feted in cities like Milan and Paris, might have said so when reminiscing about the remote flatlands of his early childhood.

The Verdi mythology starts with the date of his birth and the home in which he was raised. For over sixty years the composer told people that he was born in Le Roncole ('the scythes'), a little village in the Po Valley near Busseto in the Duchy of Parma, some 65km or so south-east of Milan, on 9 October 1814. That is what his mother Luigia had told him. In fact, as his birth certificate attests, he had been born a year earlier, in October 1813 but (according to the ecclesiastical record in the local church as well as the civic record) more likely on 10 October. He was certainly born in Roncole, but not in the house with the slanting roof which, to this day, remains the official 'birthplace' of the great man. The family *did* live there, but not until the boy was in his early teens. And his baptismal name was not Giuseppe but Joseph; in 1813 the region was still under French rule and it was another couple of years before the baby could become 'Giuseppe' in the eyes of officialdom.[4]

Meanwhile, another somewhat mythologised event occurred. In 1814, the anti-Napoleon troops of the so-called Holy Alliance pushed their rough way across parts of northern Italy, including the Parma region. Many years later, the composer told a visitor how, when a contingent of Russian soldiers (perhaps Cossacks) came to occupy Roncole, their 'outrages brought grief and terror' to its citizens.[5] Luigia Verdi took her baby son up a ladder into the bell tower of the local church to seek refuge, terrified that his crying would give them away. Fortunately, said Verdi, 'I slept almost continuously and laughed contentedly when I woke up'. Maybe. There is no evidence that Russian troops were among the Alliance armies in this region. That did not, however, prevent many early chroniclers of Verdi's life from speculating on the incalculable loss to music if the pair had been discovered – or (even worse) if the baby genius-to-be had been deafened by a sudden peal of bells.[6]

We must not read too much into the semi-truths embodied in these stories and others we will encounter later. Family records were invariably patchy in small-town Italy during the nineteenth century, and Verdi is probably no different from many of his contemporaries in giving credence to a series of questionable anecdotes passed down from one generation to the next. But two things are worth noting. First, because of the international stature Verdi went on to achieve, many of these myths soon found their way into what, until modified by recent research, was for long the universally accepted narrative of his life. Second, it becomes clear as one reads the detailed record that Verdi himself seems to have, I hesitate to say 'lied', but at least to have embellished, perhaps subconsciously, certain aspects of his personal history.

Every age has to recreate its own version of the past, seen through the agenda of a constantly changing present. We now know that some of what has long been believed about Verdi may be the result mythologisation, helped along in part by the ageing maestro himself. None of this in any way reduces the greatness of the man, however. On the contrary, the very fact that Verdi has long been regarded as one of the supreme visionary heroes of Italian unification and statehood, a genius who used his art to help better the fate of his compatriots, has itself long been incorporated into the narrative of Italian history. In what follows, we will try to separate demonstrable fact from resonant fiction, while allowing an important place for both. And, throughout, let us not forget that Verdi was a human being with his own needs and desires, fulfilments, frustrations and failings. This, to my mind, renders his achievements – as musician and man – all the more impressive.

Most creative artists are known to posterity by their artworks alone and, perhaps, by something about the lives they led. We may admire the works of Leonardo and Michelangelo, Shakespeare and Tolstoy, Mozart, Beethoven and the rest, and return to them again and again. None of these was ever regarded, in his own time or since, as a virtual embodiment of his nation, let alone a pivotal figure in its very foundation. Yet this is how Verdi was mourned on his death in 1901 and is how many continue to see him to this day.

2

Childhood and Early Career

Verdi was no infant prodigy, but he was obviously a bright lad and his parents were keen to give him a decent education. Initially, this meant visits to a friend and neighbour, a schoolmaster and sometime organist at the local church, who taught the boy a little basic Latin and Italian, and perhaps also helped introduce him to music – something for which he evidently showed early aptitude. Later, he attended the local village school. Giuseppe – 'Peppino' to those who knew him – was not a demonstrative youngster; rather the contrary. Shy, aloof even, he was 'sober of face and gesture', according to the memory of contemporaries, and tended to keep apart from the other youths, absorbed in his own thoughts and often preferring to be at home with his mother and young sister[7] (who was to die when aged only 17).

When he was 8, Verdi's parents bought him a battered old spinet which, he recalled later, 'made me happier than a king'[8] and which he kept lovingly throughout his life (it is preserved today in the museum of La Scala, Milan). Much of his spare time was spent in the nearby church where he sang in the choir and began to play the organ. He also served as an altar boy. One day at Mass, temporarily distracted by the music from the organ loft, he failed to respond to the officiating priest who angrily pushed the 6-year-old down the altar steps. Little Peppino let out a curse at the priest ('May God strike you with lightning') – and the priest duly died in a lightning storm some years later![9] True or false? It was certainly a story with which Verdi liked to regale visitors in later life, partly no doubt because it seemed to epitomise not only his love of music but also his inveterate anticlericalism.

When Verdi was 10, his parents sent him to further his education in nearby Busseto. On Sundays he would walk back to Roncole to see his family and to attend church, where he continued to play the organ. Later he recalled how, on one of these treks during the depth of winter, he fell into a ditch and thought he was going to drown until a passing peasant woman helped pull him to safety.[10]

Busseto was not a great deal less provincial than Roncole, but it was a proper town with a tradition of culture and commerce and, by this time, the *ginnasio* (secondary school) which Verdi attended, together with a literary society and a recently founded 'philharmonic society' – a large amateur orchestra that gave concerts. Verdi soon came under the influence of two men who were to play an important part in his life. The first was Ferdinando Provesi, a local composer and organist at the principal church, San Bartolomeo, who gave the boy music lessons. The other was Provesi's friend, a music-loving local merchant, Antonio Barezzi. As Verdi progressed through his teens, he would sometimes play organ at San Bartolomeo and give occasional concerts, and he began to compose pieces for the philharmonic society. Meanwhile, he was a frequent guest at the Barezzi household, the generous-minded Antonio becoming virtually a surrogate father. In due course, Verdi was invited to move in with the Barezzis, offsetting the cost, as it were, by giving singing lessons to their pretty, red-headed daughter Margherita.[11]

Back in Roncole, Verdi's parents were running into financial difficulties and it was around this time that they moved into the smaller house which the world has long thought of as Verdi's birthplace. They might perhaps have expected their son to accelerate his musical education and earning power, but the young man found himself in a perfectly amenable environment, enhanced by a growing affection between himself and Margherita. Barezzi encouraged Verdi to apply for various small grants and, in due course, for a place at the music conservatory in Milan (founded in 1807 by Napoleon). In June 1832, Verdi duly went to Milan, was tested and failed to obtain entry. The position of his hands when he played was not right, the board opined, and they probably deemed the shy but resolute 18-year-old from the backwoods too set in his ways to improve.[12] Today, the Milan *Conservatorio di musica* bears his name.

Verdi, deeply dismayed, stayed in Milan – still largely financed by Barezzi – and took composition lessons from a local musician, Vincenzo Lavigna. Lavigna, who long before had studied with the composer Giovanni Paisiello in Naples, taught Verdi traditional counterpoint and fugue techniques and encouraged him to sample contemporary musical styles by attending performances at La Scala. He also introduced Verdi to the Milan 'philharmonic', a more accomplished ensemble than its Busseto equivalent. In April 1834, Verdi and Lavigna attended rehearsals for a performance of Haydn's *Creation*. One day, the *maestro al cembalo* failed to turn up and Verdi took his place. As he recalled later, he soon found himself carried away by the music, playing with ease from the orchestral score and somehow managing to conduct with his right hand while continuing to play everything with his left. So well did he do that he was asked to direct the concert.[13]

During his time in Milan, Verdi's life continued to be a bewildering succession of triumphs and rebuffs. When his former teacher Provesi died, Verdi seemed the obvious choice to succeed him in Busseto as organist at San Bartolomeo and town music master. But a prolonged, bitter series of political intrigues led to the post being split: Verdi was invited to become *maestro di cappella* on half his old mentor's salary, while another candidate – the choice of the local priesthood – was confirmed as organist.[14] In April 1836, Verdi finally signed his contract.

A month later, he signed another: his marriage to Margherita Barezzi.

After a honeymoon in Milan, the newlyweds set up home in Busseto, not far from the bride's parents (and with Barezzi's financial support), and Verdi set out on what might have been expected to become a career as respected local music teacher, composer and occasional organist. In due course, Margherita produced a daughter, Virginia, and then a son, Icilio. Soon, however, the young couple plunged from bliss to despair as first their daughter and a year later their son took ill and died.

By now, the Verdis were living in Milan where the dogged young composer was determined to try to improve his professional prospects. Fortune seemed to smile when the impresario at La Scala, Bartolomeo Merelli, scheduled an opera by Verdi (*Oberto di San Bonifacio*), only to replace it with something he deemed more likely to succeed – and then to reinstate it. *Oberto* finally had its premiere in November 1839. It received favourable reviews and led to Verdi being signed up by the Milan-based music publishers Casa Ricordi. After *Oberto*, Verdi was invited to compose a comic piece, *Un giorno di regno* (*King for a Day*).

And still the rollercoaster ran its wildly fluctuating course. In June 1840, Margherita suddenly became seriously ill with rheumatic fever and she too died. She was 26. Verdi was inconsolable, having lost both of his children and now his wife within the space of three years. Weighed down with deep despair, he prepared his comic opera for its premiere in September. Not surprisingly, it made little impact …

There, Verdi's promising career might have ground to a halt, but for an unexpected encounter that winter in the streets of Milan. As Verdi told it many years later, he happened to run into Merelli, the boss of La Scala, who greeted the young man and ushered him to his office. La Scala it seems was due to present a new opera: the libretto had been written, but the composer, Otto Nicolai, had pulled out. Merelli pressed the text into Verdi's hands and invited him to set it to music. Verdi was in no mood to comply. Merelli was insistent, Verdi recalled, so he reluctantly took the wretched thing home and flung it down on a table where it fell open at the lines '*Va, pensiero, sull'ali dorate*' ('Go, thought, on wings of gold'). Verdi was transfixed. Before long, he tells us, the music of *Nabucco* was racing through his head.

Verdi may have dramatised and embroidered with hindsight the way he emerged from what had seemed like terminal despondency to become the most feted young composer in Italy. But the way he told this tale, in an autobiographical sketch in 1879,[15] did no harm to his reputation in a nation which, by then, was somewhat demoralised and thirsting for heroes. And there was no doubting the huge success of *Nabucco*, the opera that in effect launched his international career. It would scarcely have bothered Verdi when, a couple of years later, Nicolai declared Verdi 'a pitiful, despicable composer' with 'the heart of a donkey'.[16] The fact was that *Nabucco* – the opera Nicolai had turned down – proved to be a triumphant success. Verdi went on to compose a further twenty-five operas, many of which have remained at the heart of the popular repertoire ever since.

Nabucco tells of Nebuchadnezzar, the Babylonian king who defeated the ancient Hebrews and took them into captivity. The king believes the strong-willed Abigaille to be his daughter, but it transpires that the slave girl Fenena is his true offspring; needless to say, both are in love with the same man. At the premiere, the fiercely expressive role of Abigaille was played by Giuseppina Strepponi, a soprano who had originally been down to appear in *Oberto* but was unavailable when that earlier opera was postponed. Now, for the first time, she and Verdi worked together. Strepponi was destined to play a far more important role in the life of the composer.

And the immense and continuing popularity of *Va pensiero* – a chorus sung by exiled slaves yearning for their '*patria perduta*', their lost homeland? Many continue to revere it to this day, not just as an inspired musical composition but almost as a kind of *samizdat* hymn evoking a reinvigorated nation: when *Nabucco* is performed in Italy, *Va pensiero* is in often repeated, to ecstatic applause. In recent times, the Northern League, a political party advocating the re-division of Italy to create a new, independent northern state of 'Padania', adopted *Va pensiero* as its putative national anthem. Yet for all this, modern scholarship has demonstrated that much of the dewy-eyed political baggage that has long clung to this chorus did not really attach itself until many years after it was first penned.[17]

3

The Years in the Galley

When Verdi was starting out, Italian opera audiences generally wanted to see and hear what was new, just as today's cinemagoers prefer to try the latest film rather than return again and again to an old John Wayne or Hitchcock classic. Opera was often the only show in town, the only popular diversion in a country where, unlike Germany, France or Britain, there were few museums, libraries, choral societies or clubs (let alone high-quality chamber ensembles or symphony orchestras). Here, as at the royal and ducal courts of earlier times, the local citizenry could relish lavish entertainments that reflected back to them their own sense of social and economic advancement. And what did they see on stage? Noisy choruses advocating war and patriotism, to be sure, but also earnest advocacy of such archetypally bourgeois virtues as honour, loyalty and duty.

All this provided opportunities for an able young man like Verdi. But there was a big difference from today. We think of an opera as being 'by' its composer: *Die Zauberflöte* is by Mozart, *Il barbiere di Siviglia* by Rossini and so on. But in Verdi's time, the composer was often low down the ladder – more akin to the scriptwriter in the modern movie pecking order. 'Maestro Rossini,' said the composer's contract for *The Barber of Seville*:

> … commits himself to deliver the score by the middle of January [1816] and to adapt it to the voices of the singers; he further commits himself to make all those changes that may be deemed necessary both to the success of the music and to the convenience of the singers …

Ten years later, when the famous soprano Giuditta Pasta agreed to appear at London's King's Theatre, her contract guaranteed her not only a large fee but also the right to choose which roles to sing and which costumes to wear. Further, it included a clause asserting that Madame Pasta alone '… will choose the actors, the distribution of the roles, the absolute direction of all that which regards the rehearsals, and all else for the *mise en scène* of the said operas …' No one, it continued imperiously, 'will have the right to intervene in the rehearsals nor interfere with anything concerning the performance of those operas'.[18]

Thus the composer remained very much at the beck and call of other more powerful players in the opera hierarchy. For composing a score, he would typically be offered a one-off fee, subject to negotiation, paid once the opera had opened. Normally, his contract also required him to be present at the first three performances, directing from the keyboard, and that would bring in a bit more money. Thereafter, nothing. Many opera composers lived in penury. Even the musical score was not the property of the person who had written it but of the commissioning impresario – who could, if he wished, offer subsidiary rights to a publisher (or copyist) to print and sell some of the more memorable arias or duets. More often than not, he would not bother. And since there was still no enforceable copyright in musical scores, the most popular were frequently pirated so as to avoid rental fees. No wonder Verdi complained later that the low status and hard work of his early years as a composer was comparable to that of an overworked oarsman in an ancient Roman galley.[19]

Things were beginning to change, however. In 1843, we find the 29-year-old Verdi negotiating with the opera management in Venice over his contract for a new work. He insists he should have a say over which artists will sing, that there should be 'all the rehearsals necessary for a good performance' and that he should have the right to adjust the final scoring of the opera 'until the rehearsal before the dress rehearsal'. As for the fee, Verdi proposes that it be delivered in three equal instalments: on his arrival in Venice, at the first orchestral rehearsal, and the final sum after the dress rehearsal.[20]

The story is told of three popular composers who met in the 1840s for a drink. As they sat and chatted, they found themselves entertained by someone who, in order to attract customers, was singing some songs by these very men. When they stood up to leave, the threesome announced that they would refuse to pay for their drinks unless they were also compensated for the commercial use of their compositions. I do not know whether Verdi knew of this incident, but he was already acting as though he did.[21]

***

Throughout the rest of the 1840s, Verdi composed a string of operas, one or two a year, mostly based on the fashionable 'romantic historicism' of the time. Thus, there was an opera about the Lombards in the age of the First Crusade, while *Ernani* is about a romantic outlaw in the Spain of Charles V. *I due Foscari* (based on Byron) is placed in Renaissance Venice, and Verdi also produced a Joan of Arc opera, another (*Alzira*) based in sixteenth-century Peru and one about the invasion of Italy by Attila the Hun back in the fifth century. He also wrote *Macbeth*, the first of three Verdi operas based on Shakespeare: a brilliant and chilling evocation of a descent into evil. All these works were shrewdly adapted to the expectations and sensibilities of the audiences for whom they were written, and who undoubtedly would have experienced a frisson when, for example, in *Attila* the Roman general tries to negotiate with the Hunnish chief, declaring: 'You can have the world; leave Italy to me!'

How did the political authorities regard Verdi and all those cries for liberty, war and a 'lost' homeland (not to mention portrayals of murderous potentates) embedded in these early works? Censorship prevailed throughout Italy, from the Habsburg-controlled northern provinces through the extensive papal territories in the middle of the peninsula to the Bourbon 'Kingdom of the Two Sicilies' in the south, controlled from Naples, and Verdi's work led to a number of bruising encounters with officialdom. But his confrontations with the censors more often concerned the religious rather than the political content of his work. *I Lombardi*, in many ways a celebration of nascent *italianità*, included a big, crowd-pleasing set-piece chorus not unlike that in *Nabucco*, and a scene in which (as in Bellini's *Norma*) the chorus cries out '*Guerra! Guerra!*' In the Verdi opera this is in response to a feverish proclamation from our hero that 'The Holy Land will be ours!' What exercised the authorities, however, was a scene in which a converted heathen becomes baptised, and it was only after an 'Ave Maria' became a 'Salve Maria' that the work was allowed to be produced. *Nabucco* may have been about Hebrew slaves, but it was dedicated – as was *I Lombardi* – to a Habsburg duchess. It is thus anachronistic to ascribe to Verdi or his librettists or audiences in the early and mid-1840s the fervent political ambitions that crystallised later. Back in his 'years in the galley', what Verdi was principally doing was adopting the heightened rhetoric that was the standard theatrical language of the day, placing his operas in exotic times and locations, and lacing them with politically elevated sentiments designed to send audiences home happy.

This, after all, was what the men running the opera business (and it was always men) instructed their creative teams to do. People like Merelli knew their market, and prudent self-censorship usually ensured that a new work contained little the authorities need worry about (though the military and police would normally be present throughout, just in case). No impresario went into the business of opera with the intention of having his house closed down. Profit, not subversion, was the spur. Nor did the political authorities like to shut down a theatre – a step that was far more likely to exacerbate political rumblings than eliminate them. Even in the immediate wake of the revolutions of 1848–49, one of the first things many of the restored regimes in Italy did was to re-open their opera theatres for business, with shows that they hoped would prove popular. Once Milan was securely back under Austrian control, the authorities chose to put Verdi on at La Scala, just as they did in Naples where revolt had been brutally suppressed outside the San Carlo theatre itself.

It was not the political allegiance of a composer like Verdi that weighed most heavily with the restored rulers of post-revolutionary Italy, but his ability to fill an opera house. Here was the pre-eminent place for the ruler to display himself, fully in charge and happily smiling and waving to his subjects. So long as nothing on stage was blasphemous or directly threatening to social order, the censors could afford a longish leash. And if opera audiences purred with satisfaction at the end of the evening (and loyally applauded the monarch or minister if he chose to attend), those in government could be confident they had little to worry about.

That said, there can be no doubting Verdi's basic sympathy with the aims of the Italian *Risorgimento* – the 'resurgence' of national feeling that eventually led to the achievement of a united, sovereign nation state. The Milan in which Verdi lived was governed from Vienna, and if the Habsburg emperor wished to assert his presence in Lombardy it was to La Scala that he would go to see and be seen. From the perspective of Vienna, Austrian Italy may have looked like some kind of political unity, at least on a map. But on the ground, regional and local differences abounded. When a young Parmigiano, like Verdi, wanted to visit his future librettist, the Venetian Francesco Piave, he had to cross a series of political barriers, while an ordinary peasant from Parma or Lombardy would have found the dialect of someone from the Veneto (let alone a Neapolitan) almost incomprehensible.

All this was irksome, but you could distance yourself from your rulers by, for example, the way you spoke and wrote, and by what you spoke and wrote about. Artists and intellectuals argued about which regional dialect was the most 'correct' form of Italian, the consensus being that it was Tuscan, the language of Dante. In 1827, the Milanese writer Alessandro Manzoni published his novel *I promessi sposi* (*The Betrothed*), a wonderful and wittily spun yarn set in the seventeenth century on the borders of the Duchy of Milan and the Venetian Republic about a young couple, Renzo and Lucia, who become separated, go through every imaginable trial and hardship, and are brought together again in the final pages. The novel has many fine qualities, but one of its principal claims to historical importance is that its author laboriously rewrote the work in the Tuscan idiom, its final publication in 1840 providing one of the landmarks in the quest for a sense of *italianità* that marked so many of the cultural strivings of the middle decades of the century. The young Verdi revered Manzoni, and felt that music, like language, could be a potent embodiment of aspirant national culture. His early operas, with their rousing choruses, began to appear in Milan, Venice, Florence, Bologna, Rome and Naples, and they came to provide one of the few shared public experiences linking Italians across the entire peninsula.

None of this is to suggest that people such as Verdi, Manzoni and their counterparts in the Czech,

Hungarian and other parts of the Habsburg Empire were political revolutionaries. Rather, they were cultural nationalists: educated, liberal-minded intellectuals who valued the kind of social and political reform that they believed national, constitutional governments could bring. It was an attitude shared in other parts of Europe too: in France, Russia and many of the states of Germany. Young patriots such as Victor Hugo, Wagner or Glinka, cosmopolites all, could hardly be described as narrow nationalists. Yet they all (as did Manzoni and Verdi) created works that attempted to embody the cultural aspirations of their respective 'nations'. It may seem strange to modern eyes to couple liberalism and nationalism. Nowadays, 'liberal' thinking usually embraces a considerable degree of internationalism, of transcending national boundaries, while passionate 'nationalists' are more inclined to advocate walls of exclusion – of goods, services and unwanted people. But to Verdi, and many others like him, nationalism did not have to be destructive or exclusive. Their aspiration was for a form of government in which reasonable Italians (i.e. moderate-minded constitutionalists) governed Italians, reasonable Czechs governed Czechs and so forth.

By the later 1840s, Verdi was preoccupied with his operatic commissions and probably didn't have a carefully formulated political position other than a generalised belief in the ultimate goal of a constitutionally governed and united Italy. Then, in 1848, revolutions broke out across much of Europe. Everywhere, it seemed, nationalists and liberals rose up against unrepresentative and/or repressive regimes. In Italy, inspired by figures such as the republican idealist Giuseppe Mazzini, Austrian rule came under fierce pressure. Venice broke loose and was declared once more to be a free, independent republic. Most dramatically, the citizens of Milan managed to oust their Austrian masters during the course of five delirious days (the *Cinque Giornate*) in March. Verdi, who had been working in Paris, came back to Milan to exult in the news, writing to Francesco Piave (who was now a 'Citizen of the Venetian Republic'):

> … The hour of liberation is here; be sure of that. The people want it: and when the people want it, there is no absolute power that can resist … Yes, yes, a few years more, perhaps a few months, and Italy will be free, united, and republican …[22]

Piave had been corresponding with Verdi about music, but for the moment the ecstatic composer would have none of it: 'What has got into you? Do you think that I want to bother myself now with notes, with sounds? There cannot be any music welcome to Italian ears in 1848 except the music of the cannon!'[23]

For all his enthusiasm, Verdi soon left Milan to oversee the purchase of new farmlands at Sant'Agata near his old home town of Busseto, after which he returned to Paris. It was to be some twenty years before he revisited Milan. In Paris, he composed a new, overtly nationalistic work, *La battaglia di Legnano*, which was produced in republican Rome in January 1849 (the pope having fled) and opens with a chorus proclaiming '*Viva Italia!*'

Alas for the visionaries of 1848–49, few of their dreams were to last. The revolutions petered out and the old regimes reasserted and reinforced their rule. Pope Pius IX – 'Pio Nono' – was soon safely back in Rome, while the Austrians retook Milan and eventually Venice. In a narrow, literal sense, the revolutions seemed to have achieved little of lasting significance. Most were put down, and the surviving governments of the great European powers did their best to re-establish their authority and rule as though nothing untoward had happened. In fact, the political character of Europe was to change radically within a very few years. But that was not yet obvious. To Mazzini and the Hungarian patriot Kossuth in exile in London, to Wagner as he settled down in Zurich (where he wrote more prose than music) and to Verdi as he resumed work as a composer, the year of revolutions had provided an excess of both expectation and disappointment.

4

Verdi: In Private and in Public

Verdi may have met Giuseppina Strepponi when he and Barezzi were briefly in Lodi in 1835. But the first time he got to know her was in 1839 when Strepponi was one of the singers initially booked by Merelli for the premiere of *Oberto*. Now in her mid-twenties, Strepponi had a thriving career in the *bel canto* repertoire of Rossini, Donizetti and Bellini. This was a young woman who flung herself into everything she undertook, both professionally and personally. Perhaps unwisely, Strepponi sang well into the late stage of various pregnancies and at one time performed the demanding title role in Bellini's *Norma* six times in a week. This kind of over-activity took its toll on her energies and her voice. At the premiere of *Nabucco* in 1842, as the high-octane Abigaille, it was the dramatic intensity of Strepponi's portrayal, rather than her singing as such, that made the greatest impact. Over the next few years, Verdi and Strepponi remained friends and occasional professional colleagues, but it was probably not until 1847 when both were in Paris that they became lovers. Verdi had recently been in London for the premiere of his opera *I masnadieri*. It was not the great success he had hoped it might be and he was keen to get back to Paris to work on a new version of *I Lombardi* (to be known as *Jérusalem*), which had been commissioned by the Opéra. Strepponi, in Paris to give a concert, knew her singing days were numbered and stayed on to teach. When Verdi arrived, he took an apartment in nearby Rue Saint-Georges. The two saw a lot of each other, Strepponi giving professional help and advice where she could. When Antonio Barezzi came to Paris in late 1847 to visit his son-in-law, he was given a warm welcome by Strepponi and her students.

In summer 1848, Verdi and Strepponi moved in together. Did they intend to live together permanently? Not yet, perhaps. Strepponi was developing a local career as a teacher, while Verdi felt himself drawn back to Italy and more particularly to his own *paese*, Busseto and its environs. For all its irritating provincialism, this was the town that had moulded his childhood and youth. In 1845 Verdi had put down the first payment on a grand house on the main street and in summer 1849 he moved into his *palazzo*. Just up the street was the Barezzi family home with its happy memories of earlier days. Here, Verdi felt, he could live the reserved, dignified and very private life he preferred. A month later, Strepponi joined him.

Now approaching her mid-thirties, her voice in tatters, Giuseppina had abandoned her career as singer and teacher, evidently intent on setting up home with a man she deeply loved and admired. But Verdi was often away, supervising a premiere here, a revival there, and many of the townsfolk, aware of Strepponi's earlier career and personal misadventures, cold-shouldered her, passed by her in the street without acknowledging her and avoided sitting next to her at church. Some were more generous-minded: Barezzi, ever the kind and mature friend, retained good relations with Verdi, forbearing to make simplistic moral judgements. But one can imagine the sniggers and the giggles in small-town, Catholic, mid-nineteenth-century Busseto: hardly the place where a man might comfortably set up home and 'live in sin' with his mistress.[24]

***

If life on the main street of Busseto was not entirely comfortable for the newly installed couple, this did not seem to halt the flow of Verdi's creative energies. On the contrary, during the early 1850s he embarked on what was to prove one of the most successful phases in his career, composing three of his most enduring works: *Rigoletto*, which had its premiere at La Fenice opera house in Venice in March 1851; *Il trovatore*, premiered in Rome in January 1853; and, a couple of months later, again at La Fenice, *La traviata*. All three (like *Stiffelio* and *Luisa Miller* which immediately preceded them) concentrate less on the political themes Verdi had favoured earlier and tend rather to feature personal and family conflicts of various kinds. In particular, these works find Verdi further refining a theme which had already appeared in his work and was to do so recurrently throughout much of his oeuvre: that of parent-child relationships. *Rigoletto*, based like *Ernani* on a play by Victor Hugo, tells of a hunchback whose day job is to act as court jester to the lascivious Duke of Mantua, but whose world collapses when his own daughter not only becomes one of the boss' conquests but, at the end, dies to save her lover's life. *Il trovatore* concerns the rivalry, in love and battle, between two testosterone-packed men and memorably highlights a mother's love for her son. *La traviata* is a contemporary piece in which Verdi paints a compassionate portrait of a free-living Parisian courtesan who finds true love, but whose yearning for a stable life is shattered by the stern moral posturing of her lover's father, who insists the couple separate.

When one recalls the triple tragedy of Verdi's early adult life – the death of his two children and then of his wife – one can easily imagine why he might have been drawn, again and again, to the alternately loving yet poignant relationships between parents and children. Many times throughout his life, Verdi talked of his ambition to write an opera based on Shakespeare's *King Lear*. It was a project he was never to fulfil, but one can imagine the transcendent beauty of the final duet between Lear and Cordelia he might have composed. Among the most touching scenes in the many operas he did write is that in *Simon Boccanegra* when the old Doge of Genoa gradually realises that the young woman in his presence is the daughter he believed had died a quarter of a century earlier, and the two of them (like Rigoletto and his daughter Gilda) sing a deeply affecting *padre/figlia* duet together.

There are other themes that recur in Verdi's work. Many of his operas, for example, focus on the moral dilemmas faced by those with political power. Again and again, we encounter the irresoluble conflict between the demands of love and those of duty (or 'honour'). Yet another recurrent Verdian theme is the importance of loyalty to one's *patria* or homeland (the subject of *Nabucco's Va pensiero*). All these appear in his 1871 opera, *Aida*. At night, by the moonlit banks of the Nile, Aida, a captive slave girl serving the daughter of the Egyptian pharaoh but secretly an Ethiopian princess, thinks sadly of the *patria* she believes she will never see again. Moments later, her father, the King of Ethiopia, appears surreptitiously and presses his reluctant daughter to find out from her lover, the Egyptian general, the route his troops are planning to follow as their two countries embark once again on war. Should she obey or reject the demands of her deeply revered father? Follow the dictates of love or of duty, of patriotism or passion? All Verdi is there on the banks of the Nile.

***

Works of art can often tell us something about the personal concerns of the artist. But one must be careful not to press instant psychologising too far, particularly in the case of so rigidly self-disciplined a character as Verdi. His primary concern as a composer was to fulfil a contract to the best of his ability, and his correspondence is packed with practical suggestions to his publishers, librettists and opera managers about how best to tighten a particular scene or whom to cast for this or that role. Verdi was not a man to pour out his inner turmoil in letters to friends – or, for that matter, on stage. *Rigoletto* may be about a father grieving for the tragedy that besets his child, but it was the construction of the plot and the creative energy of the music that most concerned him.

And the censorship. The original play by Victor Hugo features a French monarch (François I) and includes a scene where the king jauntily tosses in his hand the key to his private bedroom before entering it: this sexual innuendo, plus the fact that Rigoletto hires a professional assassin to kill the king, proved unacceptable to the public order authorities in Venice who, like their Habsburg masters, had only recently been reinstalled after the revolutions of 1848–49. It was not primarily a question of political censorship (which was stronger in Bourbon-ruled Naples) but of public 'decency'. They did not like the idea of an ugly hunchback prowling around on stage or the fact that in the final scene he drags on a sack containing a dying body, and that the entire opera is about the fulfilment of a curse. Verdi and his librettist Piave agreed to make some adjustments, replacing the king with a small-town duke (of Mantua) and removing the scene with the key. But about much else Verdi was adamant. Will the hunchback and the sack cause an outcry? 'Who knows?' he asked rhetorically in a letter to the director of the Fenice opera house, adding sarcastically that the public order officers in Venice doubtless knew better than the composer of the opera what would make effective drama. In the end, Verdi got his way. *Rigoletto*, with its succession of arias and duets – and its unsurpassed quartet – proved an immediate triumph and has remained popular ever since.

The lasting success of *Rigoletto* is all the more impressive when one considers the emotional strains Verdi was confronting around the time of its composition. Perhaps his constant work served as a welcome distraction. Certainly, it frequently took him away from Busseto, leaving Strepponi to deal as best she could with the social isolation her presence produced. Verdi's parents were living at Sant'Agata at the time, looking after the farmlands he had recently acquired against the day when he himself might come to settle there.

There had been tensions between father and son before. Carlo Verdi, a devout Catholic, would certainly not have approved of his son's setting up home with an unmarried woman with a notoriously colourful past. That was nothing, however, compared with the events of early 1851 when Verdi, working through an intermediary, drew up a document stating that his parents would have to vacate Sant'Agata so that he himself could move in.

The detailed negotiations that followed are in places painful to read. A bare month before the premiere of *Rigoletto*, Verdi is taking time away from rehearsal to deny his mother the rights to the chicken yard. In the event, Verdi paid off his parents with the promise of an annual allowance, agreed to provide them with 'a good horse' and got his father to sign an agreement whereby they would leave Sant'Agata in a matter of weeks. During this tense and difficult period Verdi's mother became ill, and that summer, shortly after Verdi had taken legal possession of Sant'Agata, she died. Her son's genuine and profound grief at the news was perhaps intensified by a sense of guilt or remorse.

Throughout this time Verdi continued to work at a ferocious pace. *Il trovatore*, based on a play by the Spanish dramatist Antonio García Gutiérrez, was premiered in Rome in early 1853. With its passionate music and melodramatic plot based in a semi-mythical medieval Spain full of gypsy encampments, nunneries and battle-ready soldiers, *Il trovatore* was for many years among the most popular of Verdi's operas. The dramatic intensity and flow of musical inspiration never sag: from the introductory backstory of the woman who throws the 'wrong' baby on to a burning pyre to the final moment when she reveals to the wicked count that the gypsy troubadour and his rival in love whom he has just executed is in fact his own brother. Here are the archetypal Verdian vocal types: the lyrical, romantic tenor and soprano each with arias of yearning and of resolution; the scheming, high baritone determined to have his way at all costs; and the tough, earthy mezzo. All that is needed for a good performance of *Il trovatore*, it has been said, is to assemble the four finest singers in the world! A poor performance can be risible: the perfect example of a silly operatic plot that no one can believe, acted out with emotions so absurdly over-egged as to invite parody (notably in the Marx Brothers' film *A Night at the Opera*). The work's most famous aria, *Di quella pira!* – belted out in full voice by the tenor before he rushes off to save his endangered mother – can be thrilling if sung with confidence and authority, or embarrassing if delivered with anything less. At its best, *Il trovatore* remains an overwhelmingly powerful piece of music theatre.

So does *La traviata*, premiered just a few weeks later. Based on the play *The Lady of the Camelias* by Alexandre Dumas *fils* (adapted from his earlier novel), it is a sympathetic portrayal of a modern woman, Violetta, who is condemned by society for her supposed 'immorality' and who strives to find a deeper integrity. Verdi takes us from the energy-packed party with which the opera opens to the quiet countryside home where Violetta has moved with Alfredo, whom she genuinely loves. One day, while Alfredo is away briefly, his stern father turns up and persuades her to break off the relationship for the sake of family honour, a plea to which, with deep-felt sadness, Violetta finally accedes. She goes through the motions of returning to her old friends in Paris – but not for long, as she becomes increasingly gripped by the tuberculosis that is to kill her. *La traviata* delves deep into the erotic passions, moral complexities and powerful hypocrisies of the world in which Dumas and Verdi lived, and it contains at its core one of the most inspired (and demanding) soprano roles in the operatic repertoire. Throughout the piece there is no doubting where Verdi's sympathies lie, nor his profound disdain for the heartless morality imposed by bourgeois society upon anyone who contravenes its conventions. 'I am a lady, in my own house,' declares Violetta, with immense dignity, as Alfredo's father first approaches (much as Verdi was to describe himself, *'padrone in casa mia'*,[25] at home in Sant'Agata some years later).

Did Verdi draw inspiration for *La traviata* from the ambivalent and painful social position in which he himself had been living in recent years? In January 1852, while he and Strepponi were visiting Paris, he wrote a long letter in answer to one from Barezzi. It seems that Barezzi, long

Verdi's champion, had expressed some criticisms: perhaps of the way Verdi had treated his parents and, evidently, of his life with Strepponi. Barezzi's letter has not survived, but Verdi's reply has. For once, a man who kept the tightest control over what he was prepared to reveal about himself was stung into penning a lengthy missive. 'Dearest Father-in-law,' Verdi begins, and goes on to answer what he calls 'a cold letter' containing 'some very stinging phrases'. 'I have nothing to hide,' writes Verdi, defensively. 'In my house there lives a free, independent lady ... Neither I nor she owes any explanation for our actions to anyone.' Who knows, he asks rhetorically, 'what relationship exists between us? What ties? What rights I have over her, and she over me? Who knows whether she is or is not my wife? And if she were, who knows what particular motives, what reasons we have for not making that public?' The letter continues in similar vein, with Verdi demanding that the 'lady' in his house deserves respect, and proclaiming that he demands his freedom of action 'because everyone has the right to it, and because my nature rebels against doing as others do'. Verdi concludes by expressing his disdain for the narrow-minded people of Busseto – and with a restatement of his affection for Barezzi.[26]

The letter was written from Paris. Shortly afterwards, Verdi and Strepponi went to the theatre and saw Dumas' *Dame aux camélias*, and the following year, to a libretto by his Venetian colleague Piave, Verdi produced *La traviata*.

Here, as in his previous opera for La Fenice, *Rigoletto*, Verdi encountered the 'decency' police. Perhaps it was not surprising that the subject matter of *La traviata* raised problems. Piave had originally proposed calling the work *Amore e morte* (*Love and Death*). That would never do, so the opera was given the more judgemental title (translating as *The Fallen Woman*), by which it was to become universally known. Then there was the question of when the opera should be set. The Venetian authorities, evidently feeling that operas should feature passions of long ago rather than contemporary social problems, overruled Verdi's insistence that it be presented in modern dress. Instead, *La traviata* was performed in the safe, period costume of the era of Louis XIV.

Verdi, as was his wont, went to Venice to supervise rehearsals, only to find himself having to work with a cast who were not up to the musico-dramatic tasks his piece demanded. The opening night was at best a mixed success. Verdi called it a fiasco. But he remained philosophical. To one of his correspondents he wrote: 'Is it my fault or [that of] the singers? Time will tell.' To another he ventured a guess that the last word on *La traviata* had not yet been written.[27] His guarded optimism was soon vindicated. *La traviata* is one of that tiny band of works (among them *The Barber of Seville* and *Madame Butterfly*) which failed at its premiere but went on to become one of the most popular in the entire operatic repertoire.

5

'Viva VERDI!'

By the time he entered his forties, Verdi and his music were becoming internationally known, with invitations to compose new works or revive previous ones pouring in from across the operatic world. There were many reasons, in addition to the composer's own talents, for Verdi's burgeoning celebrity. This was the era that saw the emergence of photography, growing literacy levels, the development of enforceable copyright law and improved road networks, plus such novel modes of travel as the railway and a little later the steamship.

Verdi was fortunate, too, in settling with a powerful and loyal publisher. The firm of Ricordi, founded in Milan in 1808, had grown by mid-century to become a major international brand. Based in a wing of La Scala, the Casa Ricordi preferred to rent out operatic parts rather than sell them, thus keeping some control over performances. What they did like to sell – to all corners of the world – were vocal or instrumental reductions of operatic favourites. From these they made substantial sums for themselves and for the composers they represented. In the years and decades following the premieres of *Rigoletto*,

Il trovatore and *La traviata* aspiring young pianists, harpists or flautists – not only throughout Europe but also in New York, San Francisco, Buenos Aires, Cape Town and Melbourne – might easily have found themselves learning to play the latest Verdi aria or duet. At the same time, a rapidly growing press brought information about opera and stories about its latest star singers and composers to the notice of an ever-wider readership. All of which, in turn, helped stimulate the establishment of new opera houses and opera companies throughout Europe, the Americas and Australasia. By 1862, Verdi was able to write to his friend Count Opprandino Arrivabene: '… There is no corner in the world where – if they have a theatre and two instruments – Italian opera is not sung. When you go to the Indies and the middle of Africa, you will hear *Il trovatore*.'[28] Verdi was exaggerating of course; but only a little.

The letter to Arrivabene was sent from London, which Verdi was visiting at the time and which was one of the two great centres of opera during the years of Verdi's maturity (the other was Paris). Britain had never been the *Land ohne Musik* of caricature and mid-Victorian London could boast top operatic performers and performances, initially in the Haymarket and Drury Lane theatres and, increasingly from the 1850s, at the Royal Italian Opera in Covent Garden. London may not have initiated or premiered many of the latest operatic hits, but it provided them with a superb showcase, and Verdi recognised the importance of being known in the British capital.

He never learned to love London, however. When he first visited, in 1847, he disliked the climate, promptly developed one of his recurrent throat infections, and thought the servants 'rougher than rocks' and the food loaded with too much spice and pepper. But if gastronomical taste in London was uneven and its restaurants unconscionably dear, the city's aesthetic taste was unarguably among the most sophisticated in Europe. The main attraction of London for Verdi (as it had been for Weber and was to be for Wagner) was the money and prestige it offered. His 1847 visit was in response to a commission from Her Majesty's Theatre in the Haymarket for an opera in which the celebrity star performer would be the 'Swedish Nightingale' Jenny Lind. *I masnadieri* (*The Robbers*) was based on a play by Schiller, the writer to whom Verdi had already turned for his Joan of Arc opera (1845) and who would later be the source for *Luisa Miller* and *Don Carlos*. In the event, Lind procrastinated about when she would turn up and the opera proved no more than a respectable success.

In Paris, Verdi felt far more at home. He learned to speak and write reasonably good French and spent an aggregate of several years of his life in the French capital. He stayed there for a couple of years or so in 1847–49, with, as we have seen, a brief return to Italy in 1848; it was during this sojourn in Paris that he and Giuseppina Strepponi first lived together. He had a further prolonged period in Paris during 1853–55 and was there for about a year in 1866–67. There were a dozen or more shorter visits (some of them of several weeks' duration) during the 1870s and 1880s, and two more in 1894 when Verdi was 80. The specific reasons varied from one visit to the next, but all arose from the single overarching consideration: that Paris – even more than London in the opinion of many – was the opera capital of the world.

Paris was home to three main operatic institutions: the Théâtre-Italien, the Opéra-Comique and, most famously, the theatre (and company) known simply as the 'Opéra', based in the Rue le Peletier.[29] What audiences wanted at the Salle Peletier was *grand opéra*: big five-act spectaculars (complete with a statutory ballet scene), through-composed and sung in French by a large cast and chorus, preferably culminating with noisy and colourful fires, floods, earthquakes and general mayhem. Rossini and Donizetti launched their final masterpieces in Paris; Berlioz loved and hated the Opéra, and so, in their own ways, did Wagner and Verdi. But all knew they would not be accounted as having reached the pinnacle of their profession unless they were to achieve success here. Throughout his working life, therefore, Verdi took seriously the need to conquer the French capital: from his 1847 Parisian version of *I Lombardi* (renamed *Jérusalem*), through *Aida* (based on a French proposal and with sets and costumes created in Paris) to the ballet music the 80-year-old wrote for the Paris version of *Otello*. Above all, he wrote two *grands opéras* specifically for Paris: *Les Vêpres Siciliennes* and *Don Carlos*.

In 1855, the year of Verdi's *Vêpres*, Paris hosted a lavish *Exposition Universelle*. The city was once again the capital of an empire, the 'second' Napoleonic empire with, at its summit, Napoleon III and the Empress Eugénie. Money flowed in to fund prestigious cultural institutions and events, central Paris was transformed by Baron Haussmann into a spectacular modern city and a few years later plans were initiated for what would eventually materialise as a stupendous new opera house in the very heart of the city.

Verdi worked hard on his new opera but, as so often, various tensions intervened, notably the temporary disappearance in the midst of the rehearsal period of the lead soprano, Sophie Cruvelli. Impatient at the best of times, Verdi found the Paris Opéra rather like a vast 'boutique' with too many layers of bureaucracy impeding efficient production. Having attended the latest work by the supreme master of French *grand opéra*, Meyerbeer, Verdi declared that he simply didn't understand what all the fuss was about. He pined for the solitariness of Sant'Agata, he wrote to his friend Clara Maffei, and tried to use Cruvelli's disappearance as an excuse to cancel his contract – which only sullied further his strained relations with the management. *Vêpres* finally premiered in June 1855. Hardly the most memorable event produced in conjunction with the *Exposition*, it was nevertheless widely deemed a success.

Verdi was becoming increasingly uncomfortable with the superficial pleasures and deeper frustrations of success. Like many high achievers reaching their forties, part of him craved a more settled life in his own *paese*, where his own personal cares and values could have priority. Thinking of his farmlands at Sant'Agata, Verdi wrote from Paris that what he really loved was 'my lonely place and my sky', a place where 'I don't tip my hat to anyone'.[30] He and Strepponi spent as much time as they could at Sant'Agata, where they seem to have developed a mutually agreeable lifestyle together, Verdi nourishing his expanding estates and Strepponi looking after the home. But he found the temptation to produce further operas impossible to resist. Again and again he returned to the prospect of an opera about *Il re Lear*. Other new demands constantly intervened, however, and we find him in the mid-1850s working on an Italian version of *Vêpres*, a French version of *Il trovatore* and a new opera, *Simon Boccanegra* (also based on a play by Gutiérrez).

In the winter of 1857, in response to a commission from Naples, Verdi turned to a Scribe text (previously set by the French composer Auber) about the assassination of the

Swedish King Gustav III in 1792. The Bourbon authorities were aghast. No monarch could be represented on the stage with all the faults and frailties of an ordinary human, and a depiction of regicide was out of the question. Names and locations had to be changed. Verdi, who had gone through all this with *Rigoletto*, was prepared to make some concessions, including changing the proposed title from *Vendetta in domino* to the more neutral *Un ballo in maschera*. But he eventually fell out with the Naples management, and *Ballo* (now set, incongruously, in colonial Boston) eventually opened in Rome in 1859. By that time, the world in which Verdi lived, loved and worked was undergoing momentous change.

***

Opera composers, like most of us, tend to live in a bubble of more or less likeminded people and acquire no special expertise about the wider world. Mozart's letters show no interest in the outbreak or repercussions of the French Revolution, while Puccini was surprised and shocked when criticised for writing an opera (*La rondine*) commissioned by Italy's Great War enemy, Austria. Verdi was intellectually and politically more sophisticated. He took a deep and informed interest in international affairs, especially as they affected Italy. Like many educated northern Italians of his generation, he had been deeply touched by the promise – and failure – of the 1848–49 revolutions, and he remained inspired by the ideals of Mazzini and the vision of an independent Italy governed by Italians. When, in the later 1850s, this began to look like a real possibility, his involved interest became further aroused. Did he dream of a time when the entire peninsula might be united? Or just its northern provinces? At one stage, he seemed to favour the Mazzinian idea of an Italian republic, though when a constitutional monarchy began to look the more likely option he was to prove equally enthusiastic. The truth is that Verdi, like many of his contemporaries, probably had no fixed political ideology, but rather a resolute commitment to the broader ideal of a single nation based on a shared culture and language.

Much of northern Italy continued to be ruled from Vienna by the Habsburgs and their Emperor Franz Josef. But the Piedmont region, with Turin as its capital, was politically autonomous and governed by Italians: King Vittorio Emanuele and his astute prime minister Count Camillo di Cavour. In 1858, Cavour and the French Emperor Napoleon III signed an agreement at Plombières whereby they would jointly undertake a war against the Austrians. Napoleon III, a man with a deeply contrarian background and something of a romantic, was forever trying to reignite the glories of his uncle, the first Napoleon, and as such was no friend of the Vienna-based Habsburgs. Earlier in the year, Napoleon III had survived an assassination attempt when on the way to the Opéra. The would-be assassin, an Italian nationalist named Felice Orsini, was later guillotined, but not before he had written a letter to the emperor begging him to take up the cause of Italy. This, to the delight of Cavour, Napoleon was already predisposed to do; but he also insisted that, in return for helping Italians achieve independence, France would have the right to press its borders eastwards to include Nice and Savoy. Cavour, sensing a rare if partly clouded opportunity being offered by his powerful ally, pressed ahead with appropriately provocative military preparations, the aim being to goad the Austrians into war. Some Italian patriots, conscious that overt anti-Austrian activity could be dangerous, took to parading with Verdi's name held high, the slogan '*Viva VERDI!*' serving as a political acronym proclaiming '*Viva Vittorio Emanuele, Re D'Italia!*'

By late April 1859, Cavour's manoeuvres finally succeeded. Austrian troops were on the move and the long-anticipated war had begun. When he heard the news, Cavour was said to have thrown open the windows and burst into the opening lines of *Di quella pira!* Verdi, long suspicious of the good intentions of Napoleon III, found himself surprised and impressed when French troops poured in to help their Italian allies and he set about collecting money for the war wounded.

Things soured when Napoleon made an accommodation with his fellow emperor, Franz Josef. By the Treaty of

Villafranca, France agreed that the Austrians could retain the Veneto (and the papacy its Italian domains). Cavour argued against signing this treaty but failed to convince King Vittorio Emanuele and so stepped down from office. To Verdi and many others like him, Cavour was the one true Italian patriot unsullied by baser political bargaining. Now he was gone. Italians, it seemed, had been let down yet again by relying on foreign help. Where, Verdi asked despairingly, is the independence of Italy, 'so long hoped for and promised'? Was Venice not Italian? 'After so many victories, what an outcome!'[31] From now on, Italians were on their own.

Perhaps influenced by his admiration for Cavour, Verdi agreed with some reluctance to stand for election as a representative in the newly formed Parma Assembly. Meanwhile, at the height of all this turmoil and controversy, he and Strepponi found time to travel to a village just outside Geneva and got married. It was August 1859. Why then? Why not at some other time during their previous decade together? Indeed, why at all? Did she pressure him into marriage? Maybe it was a way of ensuring she inherited his estate in the event of his death? Perhaps Verdi, sensing his imminent emergence into regional and perhaps even national politics, felt it better to remove one stratum of potential criticism? Speculation was rife at the time and has continued ever since. Alas, as in so many of Verdi's own letters and communications, we can only resort to a series of rhetorical questions.

Verdi was duly elected. Once in Parma, he was appointed to be part of a delegation to go to Turin and report to Vittorio Emanuele. For the composer, the most memorable feature of his visit was not his meeting with the king but an appointment he had made to pay his respects to Cavour, then living in retirement on his estate. Even allowing for the extravagant courtesies of the time, their subsequent exchange of letters makes touching reading. Verdi calls Cavour the 'Prometheus of our people' and says how deeply moved he had been by the visit 'where I had the honour of grasping the hand of the great man of State, the supreme citizen, the man whom every Italian will have to call the father of our country …' Cavour in turn thanks Verdi profusely, adding that it is 'a great compensation for the hard work I have borne to [know] that I have the affectionate sympathy of a fellow citizen who contributed to keeping the name of Italy honoured in Europe'. He ends by saying he hopes he will have a chance to see Verdi 'in your native land, which is now the country of both of us'.[32]

In January 1860, Cavour returned to power with a mandate to turn the newly independent segments of united Italy into a properly functioning political entity. That spring, the erstwhile general and revolutionary, Giuseppe Garibaldi – seething with anger that Venice, Rome and the entire south of the peninsula (not to mention his home city of Nice) had been sacrificed on the altar of political expediency – led a thousand loyal followers to Sicily in the romantic hope of bringing the entire length and breadth of Italy into the emergent new nation. He was joined everywhere he went by large numbers of determined enthusiasts, and took Sicily with unanticipated ease, as well as, during the course of that summer, much of southern Italy.

All this, Verdi followed from Sant'Agata. To him, and to many northerners, the sheer bravado of Garibaldi's bold undertaking was cause for celebration; Strepponi went so far as to say she thought Garibaldi 'the purest and greatest hero that has ever existed'.[33] Others, perhaps reflecting more deeply on the practicalities of the situation, became alarmed. Where would the authority of the new nation reside if Garibaldi were to succeed in his promise (or was it a threat?) to conquer the entire southern half of the peninsula and 'present' it to King Vittorio Emanuele as a fait accompli? Tensions between the Italian south and north, with their very different histories, cultures and traditions, would be inevitable …

In the event, king and conqueror met in Naples, and the south duly became annexed to the north, with the Papal States and Rome lying uneasily between them. Napoleon III stationed French troops in Rome to protect the papacy – much to the fury of Garibaldi and others who were set on making Rome the capital of the new nation. Meanwhile, Cavour, ever the pragmatist, faced with a larger and more diverse Italy than he had bargained for, set about his daunting task of creating a manageable Italian state and the institutions by which it would be run. In January 1861, Verdi received a personal message from Cavour asking him to stand for election as a deputy to the first all-Italian parliament. It was an offer he could not refuse. In February Verdi duly took his seat in the (temporary) national capital, Turin, and on 14 March parliament unanimously declared Vittorio Emanuele to be *Re d'Italia*, King of Italy.

Verdi tried to be a conscientious parliamentarian, but his heart was not in it. 'I am a deputy, it is true,' he wrote later to a friend, 'but even I really don't know why I am.'[34] He did his best. He voted in favour of Rome being (that is, one day becoming) the capital of Italy, and he proposed state subsidies to help support the three main opera houses in Italy: Milan, Rome and Naples.[35] But his somewhat subdued parliamentary abilities and enthusiasms were further eroded by the unexpected death of Cavour in June. The statesman, one of the few people Verdi ever truly revered, was 60 when he passed away.

6

Home and Away

'Just a farmer'? Verdi repeated the mantra often enough, and was certainly something of an absentee parliamentarian. But his celebrity – and his creative inner fire – continued to prompt invitations to compose, adapt, revise or supervise operas across the musical world. In 1861–63, we find the stolid landowner and parliamentarian, the peasant drawn to his local *paese*, not only travelling to many parts of Italy but also making lengthy visits to St Petersburg (twice), Paris, London and Madrid.

Verdi's opera *La forza del destino* was commissioned by the Kamenny Theatre in St Petersburg (the predecessor of the Mariinsky). The Russians wanted grand opera on the French scale and had offered financial inducements to match. Verdi got down to work, with a text by his long-term collaborator Piave. The eventual result was a big, sprawling piece packed with love, death, soldiers and priests, an opera that contains some of the most heart-rendingly beautiful music – and unpersuasive drama – Verdi was ever to produce. *Forza* opens in a romantic, imaginary eighteenth-century Spain, and moves on to an equally fictitious Italy. The overture remains one of the most oft-performed of all Verdi's orchestral pieces, while vocally the opera includes several soprano arias and a male voice duet that are among the most deeply affecting in the repertoire, as well as the jolly rataplan of the gypsy recruitment girl Preziosilla and a finicky monk whose comic absurdity anticipates that of Verdi's final masterpiece, *Falstaff*.

The Verdis set out for the Russian capital in late November 1861 in good time for the rehearsals, with the premiere scheduled to take place a few weeks later. In anticipation of the long and demanding train journey across Europe and their subsequent wintertime sojourn, Strepponi packed everything she could think of to keep Verdi in good spirits: thick fur clothes and boots, vast stores of Italian pasta, cheese and ham, and a veritable cellar of the finest Italian wines. They arrived in St Petersburg in December, only to find that the lead soprano was ill and that rehearsals had not even started. The theatre refused to cast a replacement and, after enduring what was, both physically and emotionally, a pretty chilly Russian winter, Verdi finally had no option but to agree to a lengthy delay. He and Strepponi therefore retraced their journey, arriving in Paris from where they crossed the Channel to England.

In London, Verdi unveiled a piece you are not often likely to hear nowadays: *L'inno delle nationi* (*The Hymn of the Nations*), composed for another of the international exhibitions so beloved by the great powers of the day.

Like many other celebrated composers, from Beethoven to Wagner to Puccini and beyond, Verdi was periodically invited to compose a grand ceremonial piece to mark some quasi-political occasion. Normally a man to turn down such requests with barely disguised contempt, he had, it is true, set the words of a battle hymn, a kind of Italian *Marseillaise*, back in autumn 1848 during the euphoria of the (initially) successful revolution against the Austrians. But Verdi was in his mid-thirties at the time, and the request had come from Mazzini himself. It may seem surprising that in 1862 the mature Verdi agreed to compose a piece for the London Exhibition – though, as a deputy in the Italian parliament, he was the obvious figure to represent his proud new nation. Originally invited to compose a march, he had heard that this was precisely what the veteran French composer Auber was going to do for his contribution. So Verdi opted instead for a short cantata, for tenor, chorus and orchestra, incorporating elements of the British, French and Italian anthems. The words were by a bright young Italian poet named Arrigo Boito.

When Verdi arrived in London in April, he was furious to discover that the conductor, the Italian émigré Michael Costa, a notoriously prickly character, was not going to play his piece on the grounds, Costa told *The Times*, that it would have taken too long to rehearse and was not in any case what had been commissioned. Verdi responded in kind, icily refuting Costa's wilder claims. In a letter dispatched on 23 April 1862 and published the next day, he explained why he had decided not to duplicate what Auber was planning, adding sarcastically that twenty-five days, far from being too short a time in which to learn and rehearse his short composition, was 'sufficient time to learn a new opera'.[36] Verdi agreed, however, to attend the opening of the exhibition, at which his piece was not played, and he had the dubious satisfaction of seeing a united British press express outrage at the discourteous way their famous visitor had been treated. In May, the *Inno* was eventually performed (though not with Costa conducting) and was given warmer praise than so slight a piece probably warranted. Did this success give pleasure to Verdi? Not really. He wrote to friends how he hated writing this sort of thing, and how irritated he was when people in England wrote asking for his autograph – usually enclosing a stamped, addressed envelope, which made it harder for him to refuse. The one real pleasure Verdi seems to have obtained from his 1862 London visit was derived from the guns he bought and dispatched back to Sant'Agata for the duck-shooting season.

That summer Verdi was back in Italy. Somewhat half-heartedly picking up his parliamentary duties in Turin, he watched, with mounting consternation, as Garibaldi, ever the soldier of fortune, embarked on another adventure. Every Italian hoped Rome would one day become the national capital. But many had qualms about the confrontational methods favoured by Garibaldi who, once again, set off for Sicily to raise a force capable of marching on papal Rome and capturing the city by force. Back in 1860, Garibaldi had effectively been stopped in Naples by false northern smiles. Two years later, he was arrested by regular troops of the Italian army at Aspromonte in Calabria. 'Poor Italy,' wrote Verdi to a friend, no doubt as confused as many of his compatriots about whether to regard Garibaldi as hero or traitor. In any case, it was time for the Verdis to return to St Petersburg ...

La forza del destino finally opened in November 1862. It was an enormous success. There were hints of a demonstration on the opening night from a few nationalistic young Russians resentful that so much money and attention should be lavished on a composer from abroad. But the tsar and tsarina attended one of the performances, criticism became more muted and Verdi, for once, found himself accepting and even enjoying a succession of social engagements. Then it was time to embark once again on the lengthy return journey across Europe, to Paris and on to Madrid. Here, in the Teatro Real, alongside the royal palace, Verdi supervised an even more triumphant premiere of his latest masterpiece.

***

As the years went by, the gaps between Verdi's operas became ever longer. Perhaps there was some truth in his oft-repeated proclamation that he was 'just a peasant' or 'just a farmer'. As he and Strepponi settled to a routine on the estate at Sant'Agata, Verdi became ever more absorbed in such matters as fodder for the horses, cattle auctions, crop yields, horticultural innovations, irrigation canals and the rest. It was not a particularly beautiful part of the country. 'Nature has not bestowed any charm upon this locality,' a visitor was to write. 'The plain is monotonous, covered only with prosaic corn, which gladdens the greedy farmer but says nothing to the imagination of the poet.'[37] Nor was the climate particularly enticing. During the winters, which could be ferociously cold and bleak, the Verdis tended to migrate to Genoa where, in due course, they acquired a grand apartment which eventually became a regular second home. As for Verdi's spasmodic parliamentary duties, he periodically mused about resigning his seat and did so when his term expired in 1865. Music? New operas? No, said Verdi.[38] He had paid his dues. Now it was over to the next generation.

The fact was that Verdi had begun to feel estranged from the younger, emerging generation of Italian musicians and artists – the *Scapigliatura* (the 'dishevelled' or 'bohemians') some of them called themselves, a loose, self-consciously avant-garde brotherhood among whom were the composer and conductor Franco Faccio and the young man who had provided the words for Verdi's *Inno delle nationi*, Arrigo Boito. They had strong views and weren't afraid to express them. Their targets included people like the ageing Manzoni, whom they dismissed as a fading monument from another era. Verdi loomed far larger, especially for the musicians among them, but he was such a giant that, other than to emulate or imitate him (out of the question), they had little option but to try to bypass him. Publicly distancing themselves from the way the altar of Italian art had been 'befouled like the walls of a brothel'[39] (a comment deeply offensive to Verdi), many of them self-consciously turned to foreign influences, at first French and later *il wagnerismo*.

Verdi seemed to find congenial the somewhat isolated life he and Strepponi had carved out for themselves. They did not entertain lavishly or frequently, whether at Sant'Agata or Genoa, preferring to see or correspond with just a small number of especially close friends and colleagues. Both of them had been parents in earlier phases of their lives, but they never had children together. They did, however, adopt a distant relative, Filomena Maria, the young daughter of a cousin of Verdi's. Born in 1859, Maria (as they called her) was brought up for a while by Verdi's father before being taken in by the composer and his wife as a much-loved stepdaughter. Maria gave the couple great happiness, and in 1878 they were delighted when she married Alberto Carrara, a good local man (and the son of

Verdi's former lawyer in Busseto). A year later, the Verdi-Carraras had a child, and their descendants own the estate at Sant'Agata to this day.

Much of what we know about Verdi's inner life, his opinions and prejudices, his likes and dislikes, comes from surviving letters he wrote to people like the Countess Clara Maffei, whose highly regarded salon in Milan he had attended as a young man. With 'Clarina', as with her estranged husband Andrea, Verdi retained a lifelong friendship, albeit mostly by correspondence. It was Clarina who, in 1868, arranged for Verdi to come to Milan and meet Manzoni, by then a frail octogenarian. To the composer, who had not visited Milan since falling out with La Scala some twenty years previously, this was tantamount to a pilgrimage. Meeting the legendary novelist, Verdi wrote to Clarina afterwards, was like being in the presence of a saint. 'I would have gone down on my knees,' declared the perennial nonbeliever, 'if one could worship a man.'[40] Younger members of the Verdi circle included Emanuele Muzio, for many years a kind of cross between pupil, secretary and fixer to the great man, and the conductor Angelo Mariani. These, and a very few others, were welcome guests. Friendship with Verdi was never unconditional, however: Mariani was later to suffer the cruel wrath of his idol and was summarily dismissed from Eden.

In his professional dealings, too, Verdi was a prolific letter writer, whether giving detailed orders to those running his estates, or corresponding with opera managers or his publishers, Ricordi. During the course of a long working life, Verdi had dealings with Giovanni Ricordi, founder of the firm, his son Tito and, by the 1870s, the grandson of the founder, Giulio, with whom a genuine and professionally fruitful friendship developed. It was Giulio Ricordi who, carefully but calculatedly, helped prise open the gates of Sant'Agata to a young man who, not long before, would have been determinedly excluded: Arrigo Boito.

For all his love of life on the farm, Verdi in his fifties did not ignore opera. When invited by Léon Escudier at the Théâtre Lyrique in Paris to present his earlier opera *Macbeth* in 1865, Verdi made a complete revision, adding, among other treasures, the magnificent soprano aria *La luce langua* for Lady Macbeth (whom he referred to simply as 'Lady'). The Lyrique, a recent foundation, had seen the triumphant premiere a few years earlier of Gounod's *Faust*, a *grand opéra* somewhat in the Meyerbeer tradition, teeming with bombast and good tunes. To such an audience, *Macbeth* seemed dark and dull. Verdi had still not managed to conquer Paris.

Back home, matters theatrical continued to pursue him. The good citizens of Busseto, proud of the most celebrated figure ever to have graced their town, proposed building an opera house in his honour. This, they felt, would not only show their devotion to the great maestro but also attract the world's finest performers. Verdi's response showed the grumpy 'Bear of Busseto' at his most recalcitrant. He didn't want anything to do with it, wouldn't contribute, wouldn't attend. If they had spare cash, he asked, why not do something useful with it like build a hospital? And he recalled how, when he was a young man struggling to make a career for himself, later returning to the town with Strepponi, most Bussetans (always excepting the kindly Barezzi) had looked down on him. Why should he now contribute to the reflected glory the town hoped to gain from his presence? The Teatro Verdi nevertheless opened in 1868; Verdi and Strepponi were away at the time.

Meanwhile, Verdi had made one final attempt to create the kind of *grand opéra* so beloved of the Parisians. *Don Carlos* was one of the most opulent of all his works: his fourth opera to be based on a play by Schiller and the fourth to be set wholly or in part in Spain, in this case the land of the Counter-Reformation and Inquisition. Like *Les Vêpres Siciliennes*, the new opera was written to a French text, which, after the death of its principal librettist, was completed by Camille Du Locle, a director at the Opéra and a man who was to play a pivotal role in the creation of Verdi's next opera. The resolutely anticlerical Verdi must surely have relished the opportunity to set a spectacular *auto-da-fé* scene in which huge choral crowds watch the Inquisition carrying off heretics to be burned at the stake.

Much of the opera was composed while parts of Europe were once more ablaze. In June 1866, the Austrian Empire went to war with the rising power to the north, Prussia. It was a conflict in which Italy had a stake: a Prussian victory might at last force the Austrians to cede Venice and the Veneto region to the new Italian state. Italian troops were mustered to fight the Austrians and the entire Parma region (including Sant'Agata) was on the front line. Verdi stayed on, alternately nervous, angry and anxious, working on his opera and in his fields before he and Strepponi left for Genoa in July. The Prussian war machine, aided by Italian troops, gradually ground down Austrian resistance. As defeat began to loom, Vienna looked to Paris for help. In the armistice that followed, Austria ceded Venice not to Italy but to France. Verdi was appalled, his anger only mollified when Napoleon III passed it on, finally, to become part of Italy. 'This opera,' wrote Verdi of *Don Carlos*, 'was born in fire and flames.'[41]

The work centres on the court of King Philip II and the unfulfilled love between his son Carlos and the king's new wife Elizabeth de Valois. The lives and loves (and loneliness) of the principal characters are richly and romantically portrayed, while at the heart of the opera is an argument about the relationship between political and ecclesiastical power. Verdi spent the winter of 1866–67 in Paris, struggling with what he regarded as the Opéra's vast and obstructive bureaucracy, in an attempt to make a success of what was more or less the last of the true *grands opéras* for which the Salle Peletier had so long been famous. Perhaps it was symbolic that going up just around the corner was the immense Opéra Garnier, the theatre that would soon replace it.

Verdi found the long rehearsal period immensely trying, and was frequently weakened by recurrent throat infections. His dark mood was further deepened by the genuine sadness he experienced when news reached him that his father, Carlo Verdi, had died. Work distracted him from a tendency to depression. Sitting in on rehearsals, Verdi would place himself close to the conductor, immobile, alert, his fiercely focused eyes and ears taking in every detail. He was 'like some Assyrian god', wrote a journalist from *Le Figaro*: 'thoughtful, listening with his whole being, completely absorbed.'[42] Verdi liked to be present whenever he could to supervise important new productions of his works, often intervening in an attempt to improve not only the singing and orchestral playing, but anything and everything connected with the overall impact of the work: sets, costumes, lighting, props and the onstage positions and moves of his singers. In this, as in so much else, Verdi was a pioneer, anticipating what later generations would come to recognise as the importance of the opera 'producer' or 'director'.

By March 1867, *Don Carlos* was finally ready for its premiere. It was widely admired, though some (including the young Bizet[43]) thought they detected in Verdi's work the influence of Wagner, an opinion Verdi had to endure more and more over the years that followed. In modern times, when blessed with an outstanding cast who can both sing and act, *Don Carlos* has gained ground as one of Verdi's most magnificent creations. In Paris in 1867, rather like *Vêpres* a dozen years before, it was a respectable *succès d'estime*.

***

'Death is all there is in life,' Verdi had written to Clara Maffei[44] in the aftermath of *Il trovatore* (after some had criticised the opera as being too gloomy). Painfully familiar from a young age with the tragedy of losing those closest to him, Verdi became increasingly accustomed to the death of loved ones. A few months after his father had passed away, the man who had in effect been his second father, Antonio Barezzi, followed him to the grave. Barezzi had been ill for some time and was close to 80, but still Verdi felt the loss deeply.

In November the following year, 1868, the death of Rossini occurred. The lives and artistic personalities of the two composers were utterly different, but Verdi retained a high regard for the older man and his achievements. He proposed that a number of Italian composers each write a movement of what would become a requiem in Rossini's memory, to be performed on the first anniversary of his death. The performance was due to be conducted by Mariani, and Verdi got down to writing a closing *Libera Me.* Time ticked by and the various contributions gradually came in, inevitably creating little artistic unity. Meanwhile, with the anniversary approaching, the venue was not yet fixed or a chorus contracted. The project fizzled out. Verdi, predictably, became irritated, then angry, then furious. The whole thing was a disgrace, an insult to the memory of a great Italian. Verdi fixed his ire on the hapless Mariani.

Angelo Mariani was a violinist turned conductor and, in the latter capacity, an outstanding pioneer in a profession only then in its infancy. In earlier times, orchestral forces were generally small and could be held together by an alert first violinist or a centrally placed *maestro di cembalo* – usually the composer of the piece. Often, as we have seen, it was the singers (especially the *prima donna*) who called the shots and would be able to demand various changes from the generally accommodating composer; they, after all, were the principal attraction. Gradually, however, composers began to assert their primacy, write for larger forces and require that it was they who should decide how their pieces were to be performed. As early as 1847, an increasingly self-confident Verdi notoriously put his *Macbeth* soloists through their gruelling paces day after day, hour after hour, right up to the time the opera's world premiere was about to commence.[45]

As compositions became larger, the job of co-ordinating performances became correspondingly complex. More came to be expected of the conductor than that he merely indicate the tempo from an instrument; there was no way a work like Wagner's *Tannhäuser* (1845), Meyerbeer's *Le Prophète* (1849) or Verdi's *La traviata* (1853) could be directed satisfactorily from the first violin. So the fiddle was abandoned in favour of a baton. With increasing musical co-ordination came enhanced ambition. As conductors began to rehearse detailed matters of intonation, tempo, balance and overall interpretation, composers reciprocated by building ever-greater complexity into their scores. In the German-speaking world, the pioneers were figures such as Spohr, Weber and Mendelssohn. Italy, by contrast, was something of a cultural desert. Here, the great symphonies and chamber works of Haydn, Mozart, Beethoven and Schumann made only slow and laborious inroads (it was Mariani in 1854 who conducted what was probably the first performance in Italy of Beethoven's *Eroica*). Even in opera, orchestral and choral standards were often poor. From the very start of his career, Mariani revealed a capacity to lift the quality of operatic performance to a level probably unequalled until the arrival of Toscanini.

Verdi had known Mariani since the late 1840s. It was he who had first suggested Verdi write a requiem (in 1865, when Italy was experiencing a cholera epidemic). Verdi and Strepponi seem to have been tempted at times to treat Mariani almost like a servant, asking him to do this or that, and Mariani would typically jump to attention. Mariani not only arranged the lease on the suite in Genoa that the Verdis wanted as their winter retreat, but he even took an apartment in the same *palazzo* so as to be near them and help keep an eye on things when they were away. Was he too friendly? Obsequious? Undoubtedly, his personality – subservient, prevaricating, anxious – was sharply at odds with that of the truculent 'Bear of Busseto'. 'Don't be angry with your poor *Testa Falsa* ["Wrong Head", an epithet Verdi had thrown at him],' writes Mariani pleadingly to Verdi in one letter; in another: 'You know how I adore you and how I venerate all that is yours … Tell me what you want [re a production of *Ballo* Mariani was preparing] … and I will obey you.'

Mariani was handsome, with a touch of vanity, something of a ladies' man. Did the Verdis disapprove when he developed a relationship with the Bohemian-born singer Teresa Stolz? Hardly, given their own personal history. But alongside the emergence of Stolz as the outstanding Verdian soprano of her day, the composer seems to have become increasingly irritated by the perceived faults of the fearful and bewildered Mariani. Things came to a head over the proposed, and then abandoned, Rossini *Requiem*. Whatever Mariani's misjudgements, he scarcely deserved the cascade of reproofs he received from the composer. Worse, Verdi seems to have relished sharing his malevolent view of events with his friends: Mariani, he wrote to Clarina Maffei, 'has not lifted a finger in this affair', while to Arrivabene and Giulio Ricordi the composer complained that Mariani had failed him as both artist and friend. Mariani was crushed. His relationship with Stolz was in decline.[46] Hers with Verdi, by contrast, was soon to be in the ascendant.

The last time Mariani and Verdi met was by accident. It was 1871. Mariani was in Bologna to conduct Wagner's *Lohengrin*, the first production in Italy of any opera by the German composer. Verdi, whose growing range of irritabilities included the recurrent charge that he was being influenced by Wagner, thought he ought to go and experience the thing for himself. His plan was to sit in a box at the theatre, obscured from the public, with a copy of the score to hand. Embarrassingly, he and Mariani ran into each other at Bologna train station and had just the briefest of exchanges. During the evening, inevitably perhaps, the audience became aware of Verdi's presence and erupted into a lengthy ovation which, characteristically, Verdi scarcely acknowledged. Mariani was already suffering from the bladder cancer that would eventually kill him. 'La Stolz', meanwhile, had become something of a fixture in the Verdi *ménage*.

***

Nobody fully believed Verdi's protestations about no longer being a composer, and his postbag was full of suggestions for new operas from countless well-wishers. Many did not receive the courtesy of a reply. One correspondent Verdi did take seriously was Camille Du Locle in Paris. In early 1870, Du Locle[47] sent Verdi an outline based on an idea developed by the French archaeologist Auguste Mariette concerning love and war in ancient Egypt. Egypt was much in the news at the time. The previous year had seen the opening of the Suez Canal, for which Egypt's ambitious Khedive had invited Verdi to compose a celebratory hymn. Verdi turned down the request, but the Khedive's new Cairo Opera House was inaugurated with a gala performance of one of his operas, *Rigoletto*, conducted by his protégé Muzio. Muzio spent some months in Cairo and told Verdi in detail about the new theatre and the Khedive's intention to turn it into a major centre. The fees being offered to top singers for the 1870–71 season were prodigious as, no doubt, would be the funding if Verdi agreed to compose an opera for the new house.

The Mariette–Du Locle proposal appealed to Verdi and he engaged the writer and journalist (and onetime baritone) Antonio Ghizlanzoni to turn into manageable Italian verse the text of what was to become one of the most popular of all Verdi's operas. *Aida*, with its

French-inspired provenance, is in some ways a traditional *grand opéra* featuring bombastic, overstated loves and hates, malevolent priests, battle-hungry armies and built-in dance sequences. Like many Verdi operas, it features a heroic tenor and lyrical soprano torn between the irreconcilable demands of love and duty, and, balancing them musically and dramatically, darker messages emanating from the lower voices of mezzo, baritone and bass. Generations of opera-goers have relished the Grand March scene with its massed choruses, trumpet fanfares and optional horses and elephants. But the opera both begins and ends in quiet, reflective mood, while Aida's prayer (*Numi, pietà*) and the subtle orchestral evocation of the moonlit Nile at the beginning of Act III are musical creations of the utmost delicacy.

Aida, even more than *Don Carlos*, might be said to have been 'born in fire and flames'. In the summer of 1870, war broke out between France and Prussia. A brutal and protracted conflict led to the crushing defeat of France, the abdication of the Emperor Napoleon III, a harsh siege of Paris and the proclamation of a new united German Empire inaugurated in that ultimate symbol of French pride, the Palace of Versailles. One by-product of the war was that, as French power crumbled, Italian troops were able to take Rome (limiting the now bitter and impotent Pio Nono to the Vatican), thus preparing the way for the eternal city to become, at last, the national capital.

Verdi grieved for his friends in Paris, all the while working on his new opera about war between two bellicose states. The sets and costumes for *Aida* were produced in Paris and trapped there during the siege so that the opera's premiere, originally scheduled for early 1871, was delayed. Eventually, *Aida* was performed in the Khedive's Opera House in Cairo in December. Verdi did not attend. For him, the important premiere was that planned for La Scala, Milan, in February 1872. Here, the title role would be sung by Teresa Stolz. La Stolz knew her worth. Possibly she even overrated her value since, on being invited to sing in the Cairo premiere, she demanded an unreasonably high fee even by Khedival standards and was not in the final cast. La Scala was different, however. Here, there was no question, in her mind or in Verdi's, that she was indispensable.

Verdi probably first met Stolz in the later 1860s when she was working with (and supposedly engaged to) Mariani. A strikingly handsome, strong-jawed woman[48] with a commanding voice and stage presence, she rapidly became the soprano of choice in revivals of such operas as *La forza del destino* and *Don Carlo* (as the opera was called in its Italian-language incarnation). In autumn 1871, Stolz was invited to Sant'Agata for three weeks to study the role of Aida in detail with Verdi. It is clear that, around this time, her relationship with Mariani was at an end. So was Verdi's: barely a month after the Stolz visit, the composer had his awkward encounter with Mariani at Bologna railway station. From around this time until Verdi's death thirty years later, Stolz was to be a central presence in his life.

***

Aida at La Scala was an immense triumph, its popularity spreading rapidly to audiences throughout Italy and the rest of the operatic world. And where *Aida* went, the Verdis went. Especially if Stolz was leading the cast. First they travelled to Parma. Then to Naples where, as Verdi had anticipated, he found everyone at the San Carlo opera house incompetent or worse. While there, Stolz was briefly ill. That meant a delay in the rehearsal and production schedule. To wile away the hours in his hotel, Verdi wrote a string quartet, an elegant composition still played today from time to time, in which he called upon his early musical training. It is a characterful piece in which the careful listener might detect various typically Verdian echoes and pre-echoes. Thus, the third movement is a *prestissimo* which opens with a series of brilliant descending phrases for the first violin somewhat reminiscent of Verdi's 'Spanish' music (Preziosilla's music in *Forza*, for example, or the 'Song of the Veil' scene in *Don Carlos*). The score then goes on to include a staccato passage not unlike the gossip music in Act II of *Falstaff* and a *cantabile* 'aria' for the cello with oom-pom-pom accompaniment.

It was during this sojourn in Naples that Verdi permitted a young, impoverished Neapolitan sculptor named Vincenzo Gemito to sculpt him. Gemito produced a bust that, with Verdi's pensive head and bushy brow, was to become one of the most famous and frequently reproduced of all the many images made of the composer.[49]

Stolz, fully recovered, was again superb as Aida, and an ecstatic Neapolitan crowd escorted the composer back to his hotel after the first night with a torch-lit parade. Back home in Sant'Agata, Verdi wrote voluminously to Stolz ('Sixteen letters!! In a short time!! What activity!!' Strepponi noted soon afterwards[50]). Stolz responded in kind, though always careful to observe proprieties, using the formal second-person plural to her 'dear Maestro' and sending regards to 'dear Signora Peppina'. She became a frequent visitor to Sant'Agata at a time when, more and more, Verdi tended to lock himself behind the great gates of his estate, keeping the outside world at bay. Some people, and not only Strepponi, began to wonder about the nature of the growing friendship between Verdi and Stolz.[51] Strepponi was by now in her late fifties, just a couple of years younger than Verdi, and the early passion between them had long since waned. Despite her loyal love for him, Verdi's recurrent grumpiness and irritability wore Strepponi down at times. He was impatient with her and (she observed) brusque in his dealings with the house servants and estate staff, so that his warm and palpable attentiveness towards Stolz was all the more hurtful.[52]

In June 1873, Angelo Mariani died after a long and painful fight against bladder cancer. He was 51. His passing was not much remarked by Verdi; he had been far more deeply affected by the death of Alessandro Manzoni three weeks earlier. A few days after the funeral, the composer had made a solitary visit to Milan and had stood, silently, by the great man's grave. To Verdi, the passing of the legendary Italian novelist called for something special. And it was as his personal tribute to the memory of Manzoni that Verdi undertook to revive the idea of a Requiem Mass (a notion first put to him, years before, by Mariani).

It has been a common joke, from Verdi's day to the present, to dub the requiem 'Verdi's greatest opera'; the pianist and conductor Hans von Bülow famously referred to it at the time as 'opera in ecclesiastical dress'.[53] It is certainly dramatic. Like *Aida*, it has a hushed opening and conclusion, but within these bookends it contains powerful choruses (including a terrifying and recurrent evocation of hellfire, reinforced by mighty drum beats and chromatically descending harmonies), a *Tuba Mirum* led by spacially separated brass, an *Agnus Dei* composed as a plainsong duet, a great final fugue and, between times, a sequence of arias and ensembles varying from the sombre to the magisterial, from the ecstatic to the consolatory. In composing his requiem, Verdi in no way shed his scepticism about orthodox religion, nor was the work written for liturgical use. Indeed, Verdi's inclusion of female soloists and a mixed choir initially led the ecclesiastical authorities in Milan to refuse to sanction a church performance. In the end, the work was given its premiere in May 1874 in a church, Milan's San Marco. Verdi himself conducted. Three days later, he did so again, to a tumultuous reception, at La Scala. At both, the soprano soloist was Teresa Stolz.

The following spring, the stern landowner who had tried to shut himself inside his estates found himself once again taking to the road, this time to conduct his requiem in some of the great capitals of Europe: Paris, London, Vienna. Everywhere, Verdi was feted, decorated and applauded. In London, in May 1875, he conducted the work in the Royal Albert Hall, which had been opened only four years previously by Queen Victoria. Then it was back home – to a serene old age on the farm. Or that, at least, was what Verdi told people.

It was not serenity that greeted him, however. Far from it. For a start, Verdi had come to suspect that he had been dishonestly treated over the years by his publisher, Tito Ricordi (Guilio's father), and insisted on the right to check in detail all his contracts with the company from 1851 to the present. After much acrimony, Verdi finally agreed to accept a lump sum from Ricordi as compensation for what he regarded as unpaid commission. While this was going on, a Florence-based journal printed a sequence of articles claiming to expose details of the supposed 'intimacy' between 'Maestro Verdi' and 'Signora Stolz'. The highlight (or lowlight) was a story about how Verdi had recently lost his wallet while visiting Stolz's room in a Milan hotel as the two of them stretched out on a sofa together.

Verdi's almost permanent state of tension throughout this period, relieved by periodic bouts of fury, can easily be imagined – as can the growing anxieties of Strepponi. Most people nowadays presume Verdi and Stolz were probably lovers – though nobody thought or said so a century ago. Who can know for sure (as Verdi might have asked, defiantly)? The ambivalence, itself, is part of the Verdi narrative. Surprisingly, no conclusive evidence exists of the kind that would finally convince a sceptical historian. One can only add that, as the years passed and passions subsided, Stolz seems to have become a genuine friend and companion to Verdi, and was accepted as such (publicly at least) by the composer's loyal, long-suffering wife.[54]

7

The Ageing Maestro: Life, Death and Afterlife

Back in the 1840s, Verdi had produced one or two new operas every year. Between the premieres of *Aida* in 1871 and *Otello* in 1887, sixteen years elapsed. For most of that time Verdi, as ever, insisted he had no intention of writing another opera. It was close to the truth, but (as so often with Verdi) not quite. Among those admitted to the Verdis' inner circle was Giulio Ricordi, who would take over the family business. Naturally, Casa Ricordi was keen for him to add another opera to their catalogue, and it was the affable Giulio who, via well-intentioned guile and stealth, managed to persuade him to do so. Knowing Verdi's lifelong love of Shakespeare, Giulio 'happened' to mention *Othello* to the composer over dinner one evening, and followed it up by re-introducing him to Arrigo Boito. Boito, his *Scapigliatura* days long behind him, was now well into his thirties and an established writer, and he proceeded to send Verdi an outline of a possible operatic treatment of the great Shakespearean tragedy. Verdi acknowledged that the project had promise, suggesting Boito develop it into poetry, in which form it would no doubt be good 'for you, for me [or] for someone else ...'[55]

There things remained for several years while Verdi got on with his farming. Giulio Ricordi was keen to get Verdi to work on the project, casually sounding him out from time to time. But Verdi wouldn't budge. Apart from anything else, he said, he was under pressure to revise an opera composed twenty-five years earlier, *Simon Boccanegra*. The 'old dog' needed to have its legs straightened out, as Verdi put it, and he wondered who could best help him. Boito was just the man for the job, suggested Ricordi, and the composer and poet got down to work, mostly by correspondence with Verdi in Genoa (where the opera is set) and Boito in Milan.

The 1881 version of *Boccanegra* contained, among other revisions, a grand Council Chamber scene. Boccanegra, now Doge of Genoa, proposes a pact of peace with the traditional enemy, Venice, his plea backed up by a letter from the poet Petrarch. The bellicose Genoese senators reject the idea, calling for further warfare. The session is later interrupted by the threatening sounds of an antagonistic crowd outside but, rather than put it down by force, the doge calls upon 'patricians' and 'plebeians' alike to lay down their arms and live peacefully together. The revised *Boccanegra* was a great improvement on the original and reassured both Verdi and Boito that they could work well together. Thereafter, very slowly and with long periods of operatic inactivity on Verdi's part, the 'chocolate project' (as he dubbed it) gradually took shape.

On 5 February 1887, *Otello* had its triumphant premiere at La Scala, Milan. It was conducted by Boito's former *Scapigliatura* colleague Franco Faccio, by now probably the finest opera conductor in Italy. Among the cellists in the orchestra was the 19-year-old Toscanini.

To many, *Otello* represents the very acme of Italian opera: arguably the greatest integration ever achieved of music, poetry, drama, subtle orchestration and sheer vocal expressivity. Boito omitted the Venice act with which Shakespeare begins the play, plunging instead straight into the portside crowds in Cyprus looking out anxiously at the tempest-tossed seas where their leader, Otello, is conducting a naval battle against the infidel Turks. The opera explodes into an almighty musical storm from which Otello emerges briefly, safe, victorious and exultant. Rapidly, and with scarcely a musical or dramatic gap, we are introduced to the principal characters – notably Otello's manipulative second-in-command, Iago, and the innocent and vulnerable Cassio – all against a constantly evocative choral presence. Then tranquillity reigns as, alone together at last, Otello and Desdemona share an idyllic tenor-soprano love duet, one of the few in Verdi's entire output that is untroubled by external anxieties. These surface in the tumultuous second act, however, by the end of which the insinuating Iago, another of Verdi's villainous baritones, has persuaded Otello of Desdemona's (entirely fictitious) infidelity.

The act ends with a thunderous duet in which the two men call for vengeance. By the end of Act III, Otello has insulted the loving, uncomprehending Desdemona and is himself reduced to a babbling wreck, and in the final act he murders her, only to learn, too late, that she is innocent. Otello stabs himself. Dying by her side, he tries to summon up earlier memories and a final kiss. The opera concludes with a series of slow, unbearably beautiful, descending chords to silence.

It is a demanding work, calling in particular for a tenor capable of everything from the most melting lyricism to stentorian bravura. If presented by singer-actors capable of giving full credence to both text and music, and produced with appropriate sets and costumes by a director sensitive to all that the work involves, *Otello* can have an overwhelming impact. It evidently did so at its 1887 premiere, with the steely voiced Francesco Tamagno in the title role and the great baritone Victor Maurel as Iago. The applause was deafening, the curtain calls seemingly endless. When he finally left the theatre in the early hours, Verdi was mobbed, the crowds unharnessing the horses on his carriage and insisting on themselves drawing it to the hotel where he and Boito had to come out on the balcony and acknowledge the further bravos from the crowds assembled below. Everybody recognised that the event represented far more than merely the premiere of a new opera. It was surely the last Verdi would ever write. And it was even more than that. Strepponi wrote afterwards: 'Verdi's genius is tied to the Resurrection of Italy.'[56]

As Strepponi's comment suggests, Verdi had become a much-loved national treasure, a kind of Janus figure: the last surviving giant of the *Risorgimento* and at the same time a Moses who might yet lead his people into the better land they had long ago been promised. People pointed him out in the streets in hushed tones when they spotted him going for a walk. Giulio Gatti-Casazza (later the manager of La Scala, Milan, and subsequently of the New York Metropolitan Opera) lived as a young man in Genoa and one day followed his hero – at a respectful distance – as Verdi looked into a shop window, bought a newspaper and boarded a horse-car. Verdi was 75 at the time but looked 60, Gatti recalled, 'his head held high, his body perfectly erect and his eyes directed straight ahead'. Some years later, Gatti had occasion to meet Verdi and told him of the incident. 'What a waste!' exclaimed the maestro. 'At that age, with a good vigorous pair of legs under you, you should have been following a pretty girl!'[57]

Gradually, all the other great figures associated with the emergence of Italian nationhood passed from the scene. Cavour had died as early as 1861 and Mazzini followed in 1872, the year before Manzoni. In early 1878, the deaths occurred of Vittorio Emanuele, the first King of Italy, and shortly afterwards of the aged Pio Nono. Four years later, Garibaldi passed away, widely mourned as a national hero who, however wrong-headed at times, had devoted his life to his people. As memories of the *Risorgimento* receded, harsh new realities took precedence, a succession of beleaguered national administrations having to struggle with almost intractable problems of economic recession, widespread social hardship and re-emergent regional tensions. Emigration from Italy accelerated, especially from the impoverished south, while industrialisation stubbornly refused to take off and mafia corruption increased. Inevitably, perhaps, as people looked back with growing nostalgia to what was coming to be regarded as a golden age, Verdi, the great survivor, acquired an extra patina of heroism. In 1874 he was made a Senator for Life and in 1879 Giulio Ricordi persuaded the crusty old maestro to give the detailed account of his early life from which we have quoted. A few years later, the artist Giovanni Boldini painted what was to become the most famous of all portraits of Verdi, with top hat, scarf and piercing, unsmiling eyes.[58]

***

In the decades following Italian unification, as governments agonised over where to allocate their limited resources (squeezing what remained of local affluence in the process), opera was hardly a priority. Up and down the country, theatres had to reduce their seasons and many closed down. As for the new generation of musicians, none quite measured up. A few tried to build as best they could on the traditional Italian foundations that had inspired Verdi, while many of the more innovative sought inspiration across the Alps. 'Here is the tomb of the greatest composer of the century!' Arturo Toscanini was to write on a postcard to a friend in 1899; the card was sent from Bayreuth and showed the grave of Wagner.[59]

Wagner and 'Wagnerism' provided a shadowy, largely unspoken presence throughout the latter decades of Verdi's creative life. From as early as the mid-1860s, many (like Bizet) thought they detected Wagnerian influences as the Italian master seemed to work towards a more continuous compositional style complete with recurrent themes or motifs. Did Verdi embrace 'the music of the future'? Some praised Verdi for what he had supposedly absorbed from his German contemporary. Others criticised him for thereby betraying the very essence of *italianità*. All this was a source of recurrent annoyance to Verdi. It was not that he doubted the importance of Wagner. Far from it. We have noted the effort he made in 1871 to catch a performance of *Lohengrin*, the first Wagner opera to be played in Italy. Later, in preparation for *Aida* at La Scala, Verdi suggested to Ricordi that the orchestra be placed out of sight, adding, 'This idea is not mine. It is Wagner's and it is excellent.'[60] And on hearing of Wagner's death in 1883, Verdi dropped a heartfelt note to Ricordi. 'Sad! Sad! Sad!' Verdi wrote, adding that Wagner had left a powerful mark on the history of art.[61]

Italian and German music were, however, descended from different traditions, insisted Verdi: German music was essentially 'symphonic' and primarily concerned with structure and harmony, whereas the essence of Italian music was its lyricism. 'If the Germans, stemming from Bach, arrive at Wagner,' Verdi wrote to Faccio in 1889, 'that is fine. But for us, descendants of Palestrina, to imitate Wagner is to commit a musical crime.'[62] He said much the same in 1892 in response to Bülow who, having once lambasted Verdi's *Requiem*, wrote to say he now recognised his earlier folly and wished to proclaim his love and admiration for the man he called 'the Wagner of our dear allies'. Verdi took the apology in good stead, but he must have been riled by the mention of Wagner. '[T]he artists of the north and south exhibit different tendencies,' he wrote to Bülow, making a point of citing Wagner to the effect that all should hold on to the character of their respective nations. 'You are fortunate in still being the sons of Bach,' Verdi went on. 'We, on the other hand, sons of Palestrina, used to have a great tradition [but] it has become bastardised, and ruin threatens us.'[63]

Did the radical innovator of the 1840s become the crusty old conservative of the 1880s and 1890s? Verdi would not have been the first or last person to have made this transition over the course of a long life. Yet the evidence suggests an evolutionary process more complex and interesting. When Verdi was starting out, the opera house was primarily a place of local entertainment. Composers were often overworked and underpaid, and there were no effective copyright laws. Thus, Verdi's early operas were largely based on formulae that had been tried and tested long before he was learning his trade, with their set-piece arias and ensembles, 'big guitar' accompaniments and standardised texts and storylines. Gradually, he was able to build on these foundations and develop a more sophisticated musico-dramatic style in which voice and orchestra, text and context were more subtly integrated. Yet Verdi became ever more convinced that however 'modern'-minded you might wish to be artistically – however 'avant-garde' – you could never be truly creative unless working from within the earlier traditions you had inherited. In late 1870, while he was at work on *Aida*, in a letter turning down an invitation to become director of the Naples Conservatoire of Music, Verdi went on to pen a few thoughts about how, if he had accepted the job, he would have instructed his students to master traditional forms such as the fugue and to study the work of earlier Italian composers such as Palestrina and Marcello. He wrote about being able to stand 'with one foot in the past and the other in the present and future'. And he concluded with a characteristic refrain: 'Let us turn to the past; that will be progress.'[64]

***

To everyone's amazement, Verdi did compose another opera. *Falstaff*, another Shakespeare-based collaboration with Boito, opened at La Scala, Milan, on 9 February 1893. The maestro was in his eightieth year and it was his first comedy since *Un giorno di regno* over half a century earlier. The score of *Falstaff* is packed with musical ingenuity, the quicksilver score darting between characters and moods with a wit and imagination appropriate to Boito's cleverly constructed text. Old timers might have been disappointed that there were no sustained arias as such, while a few neo-Wagnerians doubtless nodded condescendingly at the 'monologues' and recurrent musical themes (*Dalle due alle tre*, for example, or *Reverenza*) deliciously dotted through the score. Did Verdi care? Hardly. By now he could do as he liked. *Falstaff* is something of a connoisseur's piece, never a massive crowd-pleaser on the scale of *La traviata* or *Aida*. There is, nevertheless, no doubting the consistent creativity and at times the sheer beauty of the score, while the title role has always proved a superb vehicle for a great singer-actor, from Victor Maurel in Verdi's day to Bryn Terfel in ours.

Like very few artists who lived to a great age, Verdi's skills continued to develop and grow throughout his creative life, as is miraculously evident in his two final, Shakespearean operas. And yet – ever true to his own philosophy – he brings *Falstaff* to a rousing conclusion with a good old-fashioned fugue as everyone sings joyously about the sheer absurdity of life.

***

For some years, everyone in the Italian opera world had been looking out for *il successore*. In February 1893, they found him. A week before *Falstaff* opened at La Scala, another opera had its premiere at Turin's Teatro Regio: *Manon Lescaut*, the first great triumph of Giacomo Puccini. Verdi in old age did his best to keep up with the work of the younger generation. When Puccini was just starting out, Verdi had already been sent one of his scores (*Le villi*), noting in a letter to Arrivabene that 'the symphonic element' seemed to be predominant.[65] Later, in Milan, he agreed to see Pietro Mascagni whose *Cavalleria Rusticana* (1890) he had admired. Open on Verdi's music stand, Mascagni noticed a volume of Bach.[66]

As Verdi entered his eighties, his energies, for so long seemingly inexhaustible, palpably began to wane. He was saddened by the death of many of his friends and contemporaries, while the nation he had helped to create seemed to be spiralling into ever-deeper economic, social and political malaise. He did not stop composing entirely, writing four short quasi-liturgical pieces – not because had discovered religion, but more for the challenge they offered (one was based on a teasing *scala enigmatica*). A series of photographs of Verdi, taken in 1892, show an apparently benign old man in a floppy suit, relaxed in his garden with friends such as Boito and Ricordi. The photos were in fact taken in Milan, in the garden of Giulio Ricordi, who had planted photographers behind the bushes with instructions to take pictures of Verdi when the men came out for coffee after a convivial lunch. Ricordi tried to distract Verdi, but the old man soon saw what was happening and exclaimed that he had been trapped.[67]

By now, Strepponi was recurrently ill and often sunk into depression. When Verdi finally sent his *Quattro pezzi sacri* off to Ricordi for publication, in October 1897, he mentioned as an afterword that Strepponi was 'not getting better'. She died shortly afterwards, leaving a note asking for the simplest of funerals: 'I came into the world poor and without pomp, and without pomp I want to descend into the grave.'[68] After her funeral, her will was found to end with the words: 'And now, addio, my Verdi. As we were united in life, may God rejoin our spirits in Heaven.'[69]

In his final years, Verdi devoted much of his time to charitable work. Quietly, privately, the curmudgeonly 'Bear of Busseto' had long been in the habit of helping those he felt warranted it. Ever since the early 1880s, he had taken a continuous and active interest in a new hospital built at Villanova sull'Arda (near Sant'Agata). Now, in extreme old age, he also undertook what he talked of as the finest of all his creations: the Casa di Riposo, a home for retired musicians in Milan, designed by Camillo Boito, the architect brother of Arrigo. This, Verdi stipulated in his will, was where his royalties were to be paid after his death.

On 27 February 1901, Verdi's body was finally laid to rest here, together with that of Strepponi. One parliamentarian, mourning Verdi's passing, declared him to have been 'the symbol of the heroic era of our Risorgimento because of the mystic fusion of his music and the longed-for, prayed-for unity of our nation'.[70] The patriotic poet Gabriele d'Annunzio was to go further, penning an ode in which he declared, 'We were nourished by him as by bread'. This was not far short of transubstantiation.

Deeply and sincerely though Verdi was mourned, much of his oeuvre had, by the end of his life, come to be regarded as passé. While people revered him for the *patria* and *libertà* hymned in some of his works, it was the man almost more than the music that Italians celebrated in the early years of the new century. Wagner's operas were more popular than most of Verdi's, even in Italy. True, a handful of Verdi's mid-career masterpieces continued to hold the stage, but audiences would flock to *I Maestri Cantori di Nurembergo* or *L'Oro del Reno* rather than sit through *Falstaff* or the 'oom-pom-pom' of *Nabucco* or *Attila*. In 1913, the centenary of Verdi's birth, many cities across Italy held celebratory events, none more extravagant than the great exhibition mounted in Parma to honour the memory of the duchy's favourite son. Music was played of course. But the exhibition mostly celebrated Verdi's 'peasant origins', his love of the land and how, after his various artistic battles, he 'loved to restore himself in the serene vision of his countryside'.[71]

In the 1920s, with the advent of Mussolini, Verdi was held up primarily as a national hero, a great patriot.

Ironically, it was the German world that pioneered the Verdi renaissance from which we still benefit today. The writer Franz Werfel wrote a novel about Verdi, adapted a number of his libretti and issued an edition of his letters, while the director Carl Ebert and conductor Fritz Busch (later the founding artistic directors of Glyndebourne) pioneered revivals of his lesser known operas such as *Forza*, *Macbeth* and *Ballo* in the 1920s and early 1930s. Nor was Verdi's appeal diminished under Nazism. If anything it was enhanced as the great man's stolid patriotism was enlisted along with his charitable activities and his love of the soil. As the Reich forged closer relations with Fascist Italy, performances of Verdi multiplied, outnumbering those of Wagner.[72]

Today, as we saw at the outset of this book, the works of Verdi lie at the very heart of the operatic repertoire, receiving more performances across the world than those of any other composer. During the 2011–12 season, for example, a total of 3,020 Verdi productions were scheduled worldwide, with Mozart coming a distant second (2,410), followed by Puccini (2,294) and then Wagner (1,292).[73] As for Verdi himself, he continues to be revered, not only as a supreme artistic genius but also as a great man and a deeply honoured patriot. As Italy struggles once more to find its way through its recurrent woes, the operas of Verdi, and the collective memory of the exemplary figure who created them, continue to inspire. *Viva VERDI!*

Notes

All details about Verdi's life are derived from primary sources, most of them cited in the books listed under Further Reading, and noted accordingly. Notes do not include comprehensive references to academic and other articles, while the broader historical context (some of which is also covered in my book *The Gilded Stage: A Social History of Opera*) is derived from a far more extensive range of sources than can be listed here.

1   See Williams, Gavin, 'Orating Verdi: Death and the media c.1901', in *Cambridge Opera Journal*, Vol. 23, Issue 3, November 2011, pp. 119–43.

2   Rosselli, John, *The Life of Verdi* (CUP, 2000), p. 12; Phillips-Matz, Mary Jane, *Verdi: A Biography* (OUP, 1993), p. 520.

3   *The Life of Verdi*, ibid., pp. 12, 15.

4   *Verdi: A Biography*, op. cit., pp. 11–2; Martin, George, *Verdi, His Music, Life and Times* (Macmillan, 1963), p. 3.

5   Conati, Marcello (ed.), *Interviews and Encounters with Verdi* (Gollancz, 1984), p. 151; *Verdi: A Biography*, pp. 13–4.

6   Ibid.

7   *Verdi: A Biography*, op. cit., p. 17.

8   *Interviews and Encounters with Verdi*, op. cit., p. 150; ibid., p. 18.

9   *Verdi: A Biography*, op. cit., p. 19.

10 *Interviews and Encounters with Verdi*, op. cit., p. 150.

11 For a portrait of Antonio Barezzi, see http://commons.wikimedia.org/wiki/File:Ritratto_di_Antonio_Barezzi.jpg; for Margherita Barezzi, see http://scuolallopera.files.wordpress.com/2012/10/marghe.jpg.

12 *Verdi: A Biography*, op. cit., pp. 43–5.

13 Ibid., p. 50.

14 Ibid., pp. 54–75 passim.

15 In his later years, Verdi gave a number of (no doubt equally embroidered) versions of the origins of *Nabucco*; ibid., pp. 106–8.

16 Budden, Julian, *The Operas of Verdi*, Vol. 1 (OUP, 1973), p. 93.

17 See, for example, Parker, Roger, *Leonora's Last Act* (Princeton University Press, 1997), chapter 2. Also Parker's 2007 Gresham College lecture (www.gresham.ac.uk/lectures-and-events/verdi-and-milan).

18 For the Rossini contract, see Cagli, Bruno, 'Verdi and the Business of Writing Operas', in Weaver, William & Chusid, Martin (eds), *The Verdi Companion* (W.W. Norton & Co., 1979), p. 114, note 12. For

the Pasta contract, see Rutherford, Susan, *The Prima Donna and Opera: 1815–1930* (CUP, 2007), pp. 167–8.

19 Letter to Clara Maffei, 12 May 1858.

20 'Verdi and the Business of Writing Operas', op. cit., p. 113.

21 Sassoon, Donald, *The Culture of the Europeans: From 1800 to the Present* (HarperCollins, 2006), p. 508. The anecdote also appears (featuring a single composer) in Roth, Ernst, *The Business of Music: Reflections of a Music Publisher* (Cassell, 1969), p. 33.

22 *Verdi: A Biography*, op. cit., pp. 230–1.

23 Ibid.

24 For more detail about Strepponi, see Walker, Frank, *The Man Verdi* (University of Chicago Press, 1982), chapter 7, and Servadio, Gaia, *The Real Traviata: Biography of Giuseppina Strepponi, Wife of Giuseppe Verdi* (Hodder & Stoughton, 1994).

25 *Verdi: A Biography*, op. cit., p. 296.

26 Osborne, Charles (ed.), *Letters of Giuseppe Verdi* (Gollancz, 1971), pp. 82–4.

27 *Verdi: A Biography*, op. cit., p. 323.

28 Ibid., p. 449.

29 The present Opéra, much of it built during the 1860s, opened in 1875, two years after the Salle Peletier burned down. A fourth opera company, the Théâtre Lyrique, flourished during the 1850s and 1860s.

30   *Verdi: A Biography*, op. cit., p. 340.

31   Ibid., p. 394.

32   *Verdi, His Music, Life and Times*, op. cit., pp. 304–5;
ibid., p. 401.

33   *Verdi: A Biography*, op. cit., p. 423.

34   Ibid., p. 430.

35   *Verdi, His Music, Life and Times*, op. cit., p. 317.

36   *The Times*, letters, 24 April 1862.

37   *Interviews and Encounters with Verdi*, op. cit.,
p. 71.

38   'I no longer compose', Verdi repeated several times
to a visiting impresario in 1859; ibid., p. 38.

39   *Verdi: A Biography*, op. cit., p. 468; *Verdi, His Music,
Life and Times*, op. cit., p. 338; *The Man Verdi*, op.
cit., p. 449; *The Life of Verdi*, op. cit., p. 126.

40   *Verdi, His Music, Life and Times*, ibid., p. 366; *Verdi:
A Biography*, ibid., p. 547.

41   *Verdi: A Biography*, ibid., p. 514.

42   Ibid., p. 519; *Interviews and Encounters with Verdi*,
op. cit., p. 61.

43   *Verdi: A Biography*, ibid., p. 521.

44   *Verdi, His Music, Life and Times*, op. cit., p. 250; ibid.,
p. 309.

45   *Interviews and Encounters with Verdi*, op. cit.,
pp. 26–7.

46   Verdi's relationship with Mariani is dealt with in
detail in *The Man Verdi*, op. cit., chapter 7.

47   In 1870, Du Locle left the Opéra to take over
      co-directorship of the Opéra-Comique where, a few
      years later, he produced Bizet's new opera *Carmen*.

48   See, for example: http://hu.wikipedia.org/wiki/
      F%C3%A1jl:Teresa-Stolz.jpg.

49   See: http://www.copia-di-arte.com/a/gemito-
      vincenzo/bust-of-guiseppe-verdi-18.html.

50   *Verdi: A Biography*, op. cit., p. 597.

51   Ibid., p. 598.

52   For details of the growing tensions between Verdi
      and Strepponi, see *The Man Verdi*, op. cit., chapter 8.

53   Walker, Alan, *Hans von Bülow: A Life and Times*
      (OUP, 2010), pp. 195–6.

54   Further details about the relationship between Verdi
      and Stolz are included in *The Man Verdi*, op. cit.,
      chapter 8.

55   *Letters of Giuseppe Verdi*, op. cit., p. 209.

56   *Verdi: A Biography*, op. cit., pp. 688–9.

57   Gatti-Casazza, Giulio, *Memories of the Opera* (John
      Calder, 1977), pp. 34–5.

58   http://www.theseekermagazine.com/wp-content/
      uploads/Giuseppe-Verdi-Boldini.jpg.

59   Sachs, Harvey, *Toscanini* (J.B. Lippincott Co., 1978),
      p. 72.

60   *Verdi: A Biography*, op. cit., p. 583.

61   *Letters of Giuseppe Verdi*, op. cit., p. 219.

62   Ibid., pp. 239–40.

63 *Hans von Bülow: A Life and Times*, op. cit.,
    pp. 429–30; ibid., p. 249. Bülow's comment about
    'our dear allies' refers to the Triple Alliance between
    Germany, Austria-Hungary and Italy, 1882–1914.

64 *Letters of Giuseppe Verdi*, ibid., pp. 168–9.

65 *Verdi: A Biography*, op. cit., p. 677.

66 *Interviews and Encounters with Verdi*, op. cit., p. 314.

67 Ibid., pp. 225–7.

68 *Verdi: A Biography*, op. cit., pp. 741–2.

69 Ibid., p. 743.

70 Ibid., p. 762.

71 On the Verdi centenary exhibition, see Basini, Laura,
    'Cults of Sacred Memory: Parma and the Verdi
    centennial celebrations of 1913', in *Cambridge Opera
    Journal*, Vol. 13, Issue 3, pp. 141–61, 2001.

72 For detailed figures, see Levi, Erik, *Music in the Third
    Reich* (Macmillan, 1994), pp. 192–3. On Werfel and
    the 'Verdi Renaissance', see Martin, George, *Aspects of
    Verdi* (Robson Books, 1988), chapter 3. On the Verdi
    revival in Germany more generally, see Kreuzer,
    Gundula, *Verdi and the Germans: From Unification to
    the Third Reich* (CUP, 2010), chapters 4, 5.

73 Statistics derived from www.operabase.com.

Timeline

1813	10 October: born, Le Roncole
1823	To Busseto to study at Ginnasio
1824	Begins music studies with Ferdinando Provesi
1832	To Milan; fails to gain admission to the *conservatoire*; begins private studies with Vincenzo Lavigna
1836	4 May: marries Margherita Barezzi
1837	26 March: daughter Virginia born
1838	11 July: son Icilio born 12 August: death of Virginia
1839	The Verdis move back to Milan; Verdi meets Giuseppina Strepponi 22 October: death of Icilio 17 November: *Oberto, Conte di San Bonifacio* (La Scala, Milan). The Milan publisher Casa Ricordi secures rights to his next work
1840	18 June: death of Margherita 5 September: *Un giorno di regno* (La Scala, Milan)

1842	9 March: *Nabucco*; Giuseppina Strepponi sings Abigaille
1843	11 February: *I Lombardi alla prima crociata* (La Scala, Milan)
1844	9 March: *Ernani* (Venice) 3 November: *I due Foscari* (Rome)
1845	15 February: *Giovanna d'Arco* (La Scala) 12 August: *Alzira* (Naples)
1846	17 March: *Attila* (Venice)
1847	14 March: *Macbeth* (Florence) 22 July: *I masnadieri* (London) 26 November: *Jérusalem* (Paris); buys farmlands at Sant'Agata; relationship with Strepponi develops in Paris
1848	Revolutions across Europe March: *Cinque giornate* April/May: visits Milan then Busseto and Sant'Agata before returning to Paris; lives in Passy with Strepponi 25 October: *Il corsaro* (Trieste)
1849	27 January: *La battaglia di Legnano* (Rome) July: leaves Paris to live in Busseto, where Strepponi joins him in September 8 December: *Luisa Miller* (Naples)
1850	16 November: *Stiffelio* (Trieste)
1851	January–April: tensions between Verdi and his parents

	11 March: *Rigoletto* (Venice)
	May: Verdi and Strepponi move to Sant'Agata
	28 June: death of Verdi's mother
1853	19 January: *Il trovatore* (Rome)
	6 March: *La traviata* (Venice)
1855	13 June: *Les vêpres siciliennes* (Paris)
1857	12 March: *Simon Boccanegra* (Venice)
	16 August: *Aroldo* (revision of *Stiffelio*, Rimini)
1859	17 February: *Un ballo in maschera* (Rome)
1859–61	*Risorgimento* culminates in Italian unification and statehood
1859	29 August: Verdi and Strepponi marry
1861	18 February: Verdi sworn in as a deputy in the first all-Italian parliament (Turin)
1862	April/May: *Inno delle nazioni* (London)
	10 November: *La forza del destino* (St Petersburg)
1865	21 April: revised *Macbeth* (Paris)
1867	14 January: death of Verdi's father
	11 March: *Don Carlos* (Paris)
	21 July: death of Antonio Barezzi; Verdi and Strepponi adopt Filomena Maria Verdi as foster daughter
1868	Visits Milan and meets Manzoni
1869	Opening of Suez Canal and Cairo opera house

1870–71	Franco-Prussian War
1871	18 January: German Empire declared
	1 July: Rome becomes capital of Italy
	19 November: hears *Lohengrin* in Bologna
	24 December: *Aida* (Cairo)
1872	8 February: *Aida* premiered at La Scala with Stolz in title role
1873	String quartet; death of Manzoni
1874	22 May: *Requiem* (Milan)
1875	Conducts *Requiem* in Vienna and London; extends estates with further purchases
1878	Filomena Maria Verdi marries Alberto Carrara
1881	24 March: *Simon Boccanegra* (revised version; La Scala)
1883	13 February: death of Wagner in Venice
1887	5 February: *Otello* (La Scala)
1888	Inauguration of hospital built by Verdi at Villanova sull'Arda
1893	1 February: Puccini's *Manon Lescaut* (Turin)
	9 February: *Falstaff* (La Scala)
1895	Inauguration of Casa di Riposo project
1897	Sends *Quattro pezzi sacri* to Ricordi for publication (1898)
	14 November: death of Strepponi
1901	27 January: death of Verdi (Milan)
	27 February: Verdi and Strepponi reinterred at Casa di Riposo, Milan

Further Reading

English language accounts of Verdi's life:
Budden, Julian, *Verdi* (Dent, revised edn 1993)
Martin, George, *Verdi, His Music, Life and Times*
    (Macmillan, 1963)
Meier, Barbara, *Verdi* (Haus Publishing, 2003)
Phillips-Matz, Mary Jane, *Verdi: A Biography* (OUP, 1993)
Rosselli, John, *The Life of Verdi* (CUP, 2000)

Insights into Verdi's personal relationships:
Conati, Marcello (ed.), *Interviews and Encounters with*
    Verdi (Gollancz, 1984)
Servadio, Gaia, *The Real Traviata: Biography of Giuseppina*
    Strepponi, Wife of Giuseppe Verdi (Hodder &
    Stoughton, 1994)
Walker, Frank, *The Man Verdi* (University of Chicago
    Press, 1982)

Verdi the composer:
Balthazar, Scott L. (ed.), *The Cambridge Companion to*
    Verdi (CUP, 2004)
Budden, Julian, *The Operas of Verdi*, 3 vols (OUP, 1973–81)

Parker, Roger, *'New Grove' Guide to Verdi and his Operas* (OUP, 2007)

Parker, Roger, *Leonora's Last Act: Essays in Verdian Discourse* (Princeton University Press, 1997)

Containing Verdi-related essays and documents:

Martin, George, *Aspects of Verdi* (Robson Books, 1988)

Osborne, Charles (ed.), *Letters of Giuseppe Verdi* (Gollancz, 1971)

Weaver, William (ed.), *Verdi: A Documentary Study* (Thames & Hudson, 1977)

Weaver, William & Chusid, Martin (eds), *The Verdi Companion* (W.W. Norton & Co., 1979)

Web Links

There are countless online resources available in English for the Verdi admirer. Many reiterate or illustrate the biographical material above or outline details of particular works or performances. Some are more substantial without being too arcane or academic for the general reader.

http://www.studiverdiani.it/verdi_en.html – Notably
    accessible to the general reader

http://www.oxfordmusiconline.com/public/book/omo_
    gmo – The most thorough and authoritative online
    coverage of Verdi and his operas is Grove Music
    Online (for which a subscription is required)

http://verdisdisco.de/ – For details of recordings of works
    by Verdi

http://www.operadis-opera-discography.org.uk/
    CLORVERD.HTM – As above

Giuseppe Verdi Henry V **Brunel** Pope John Paul II **Jane Austen** William the Conqueror **Abraham Lincoln** Robert the Bruce **Charles Darwin** Buddha **Elizabeth I** Horatio Nelson **Wellington** Hannibal & Scipio **Jesus** Joan of Arc **Anne Frank** Alfred the Great **King Arthur** Henry Ford **Nelson Mandela**